# IS YOUR CHILD IN
# THE WRONG GRADE?

*Other Gesell Institute Books*

# *Is Your*
# *Child in the*
# WRONG
# GRADE ?

---

## Louise Bates Ames, Ph.D.

GESELL INSTITUTE OF CHILD DEVELOPMENT

*With a Preface by* FRANCES L. ILG, *M.D.*

## HARPER & ROW, PUBLISHERS

*New York, Evanston, and London*

# CONTENTS

# PREFACE

There was a time in the earlier years of our nation when we seemed instinctively to be moving in the right direction in the education facilities provided for and demands made of our children. But modern, rapid, machinelike concepts have made us, temporarily we hope, take a wrong turn. We have been lured by the streamlined potentials and shiny superficiality and rapidity of machine production. We have all too often neglected to include in our thinking and planning the more intricate, slower, irregular and vital processes of biological growth.

Thus we have unknowingly deprived many of our children of the joy, fun and choice of growing through their own inner growth urges, which are sizeable. Rather have we imposed often valueless or misplaced goals upon them, with the resulting compensating tensions. The intellectual diet we have given children under pressure has produced its predictable indigestion, resistance, blackout and even breakdown.

This book speaks most clearly and directly to parents, both to support the already concerned parent and to alert the parent who is less aware. The child reveals himself most clearly and fully in his home. May this book give the parent confidence to impart his knowledge and instinctive feeling about his child to the school. But may the school also be rewarded with a receptive and understanding parent. The child needs both home and school. May each ones greater knowledge of growth forces help him to enter into a more effective partnership for the greater good of every child.

—Frances L. Ilg, M.D.

*New Haven, Connecticut*

## PART ONE

# Every Child Correctly Placed

# Chapter 1

## IS YOUR CHILD IN

## THE WRONG GRADE?

IS your child in the wrong grade? Chances are that he may be. Research conducted at the Gesell Institute in the past ten years reveals that at least one child in three may definitely be overplaced and struggling with the work of a grade which is really beyond his ability. The figure may be even larger.

Most school systems in the United States require that a child be five by some certain date before he starts kindergarten, six before he starts first grade. Even when this cut-off date is September first, which does fairly well for most girls, it results in many boys (who as a rule develop a little more slowly than girls) being too young for the grade in which age places them. And all too often a child is allowed to start first grade when he will not be six till November or December or even January, so that in all too many communities a child can start first grade at the unreasonably early age of five-and-a-half years.

Our findings have been that so long as the kindergarten and first grade curriculums remain more or less as they are in our school systems, the average girl needs to be fully five before starting kindergarten, the average boy fully five-and-a-half.

We also find, and this will be news to some—especially to those state legislatures which rule that children are ready to start school when they have reached a certain chronological age—that it is not the child's age in years which proves the best clue as to whether or not he is ready for the work of any given grade. Instead, actual practice shows that the very best measure of readiness for the work of any grade is not age in years but, rather, behavior age. Behavior age means just what it sounds like. It means the age at which a child is behaving.

Thus a boy or girl could be seven years old, yet if in general ways he is behaving like a five-year-old, he belongs in kindergarten with other five-year-olds, not in second grade where the law of many states would place him. Fortunately it is now quite easy and possible to determine behavior age by relatively simple tests which we shall tell you about later in this book. Today it is fully possible for parents and teachers and school administrators to find out just what any given child's behavior age is.

If we must choose an arbitrary calendar age, many people are beginning to believe that the age of seven might be better than six for starting first grade. We prefer, however, that it be the child's behavior and not his age in years which should decide his readiness for starting school. We propose that each child, before school entrance, be given an individual behavior test which could tell us, and tell you, whether or not he is ready for the work and activities of the usual kindergarten or first grade, as the case may be.

There is the story of the little first-grader who, when asked by her father one spring day what they had done in school that day, replied: "We planted seeds in plant pots to see if they would grow. But we ran out of dirt so the teacher let me go out in the yard to get some more dirt. And, Daddy, I was out there *all alone*. I could have escaped."

It's a wonder to us that more children don't escape, or at least try to escape, when we consider how many of them today are placed in a grade which is far beyond their ability and maturity level. And actually many of them do escape. Perhaps not literally. They go to school every day and sit in the seat assigned to them. They escape by not doing the work required, by not "behaving" in class, by daydreaming, by looking out the window, by not holding up physically and emotionally in the classroom and/or at home.

We have long been aware of the fact that many, many children in the schools today are not up to the work that is being expected of them. However, even with all the evidence staring us in the face, we did not at first see the full implications of what we observed. Way back in the 1940's we were doing research for our book *The Child from Five to Ten* by Gesell and Ilg (Harper). We observed that very few of our research subjects, five-to ten-year-old New Haven children of rather high intellectual and socio-economic status, were actually up to the curriculum requirements of the grades they were in.

At that time we interpreted it that the curriculums put out by most state departments of education were unrealistic, being beyond the ability of even the superior child. But even with our developmental slant, we failed to see the implications of what we were observing. It's true of course that the curriculum of each grade, all along, *could* be reduced way down to what the children were able to perform.

Curriculums admittedly do need to be improved. But since the body of knowledge which must be covered in the schools today is greater than ever, it now seems to us more realistic and effective to work on the *other* variable—the child's ability to perform. Rather than setting the over-all curriculum back a grade all along the way, twenty more years of work in education have led us to the conclusion that the best solution, rather than shifting the whole curriculum downward to meet the child's immaturity, would be to check and see that each child was ready for what each of the various grades demands.

Even more than our research experience, it was our own clinical experience which alerted us to the tremendous amount of overplacement in our schools today. In the past ten years or so we have noted that nearly all of the children brought to us because of school problems were overplaced. That is, they were placed in a grade above that which their maturity level suited them for, in a grade above the one where they could actually do the work.

And so, we came to ask ourselves the question—is this high degree of overplacement true of children in general, or does it hold true just in the cases of children who have gotten into enough trouble in school to be brought to a children's clinic?

To answer this question, we carried out a three-year-long research study* in the Hurlbutt School in Weston, Connecticut, giving our Gesell Behavior Examination to all of the children in the kindergarten, and in one first-grade and one second-grade class, in the fall of 1957 and examining all of these same children again in 1958 and 1959.

Results of this testing were rather shocking. According to our evaluation, for the kindergarten group only 37 percent of the children (approximately one third) were fully ready for the work of kindergarten and to be promoted to first grade the following year. Forty-three percent were questionably ready for kindergarten and definitely not ready to be promoted to first grade the following year. Twenty percent were definitely unready for kindergarten.

Findings for first- and second-graders were approximately the same. In each of these classes, only about one third of the children were ready for the work of the grade in which age had placed them; just over one third were questionably ready (that is they might make it but were not securely ready). Just under one third were definitely unready.

A second important finding was that unready children did not, in succeeding years, "catch up" with the ready ones. Parents and teachers alike often phrase the hopeful comment, "True, he's a little bit immature right now, but he's bound to catch up." Most unready children do not, in our experience, catch up. If growth is proceeding at an "average" rate, a child's behavior grows about a year in one year's time. But it does not as a rule grow more than a

* Generous support for this study as well as for subsequent work in this field of school readiness, including present demonstration projects in schools in Bennington, Vermont, Cheshire, Connecticut, and Visalia, California, was supplied by the Fund for the Advancement of Education of the Ford Foundation.

year in one year, and it would have to do that if the child were going to "catch up."

A third question which our research answered was: To what extent could we on the basis of a twenty-minute behavior test given in the fall of a school year predict what the teacher would have to say of each child's performance come June? That is, could we, in the fall of the year, predict which children would not "pass" in June?

There turned out to be a high correlation between fall predictions and June evaluations. Correspondence was highest for the kindergarten children. There was 83 percent agreement between our predictions about school performance and what the teacher felt about the child's performance during the school year. In nearly every instance we had been able to predict sure failure and sure success. It was only in the case of a few of the "questionable" children that our prediction and the teacher's verdict differed.

Our conclusion at the end of three years of research in this rather typical public school was, therefore, that age alone is not an adequate basis for determining the time of school entrance, and that many children legally old enough to begin school are not old enough in their behavior to do so. Your own boy or girl may be such a child.

Though it is never too late to hold back a child who has been started too soon, it's better yet to avoid the whole problem of overplacement by having each child start school on the basis of his behavior age rather than his age in years. We hope that this book will help in both cases—help to prevent children starting too soon; help encourage parents to replace children who are now overplaced.

Another hazard presents itself in some communities. If a child has a high enough Intelligence Quotient, or if he reads at a first-grade level, he can be entered in school even though he falls below the age requirement. Our experience in Weston and elsewhere has led us to believe that a high I.Q. or above average reading ability, unless it is supported by a total performance (behavior level) which is fully at age, is no more effective than legal age in guaranteeing success in school.

As we shall point out in the pages which follow, we do not agree with those parents and those educators who feel that most children fail in school because they do not try. We have never agreed with the all too familiar phrase, "He *could* do better if he would." Our version is, instead, "He *would* do better if he *could.*"

Similarly, in most instances we question the concept of "underachievement." People talk a lot about underachievers. The word implies that the child could do better, has the capability of doing better, than he actually is doing. And when pinned down, the people who use this term usually turn out to mean that the child in question has a high I.Q. and therefore they assume that he is capable of a better academic performance than he is giving. In our experience, a high I.Q. is no guarantee of adequate school performance, and most children, much of the time, do the best they can.

Now just one word about school drop-outs, that unfortunate group of boys and girls who so often handicap themselves for their entire lives because they do not have the stamina, ability or good fortune to stay in school till they have completed high school. Much work has been done on the drop-out problem at the high-school level, in efforts to get these drop-out children to go back to school.

In our opinion, the drop-out problem begins long before most children actually do their dropping out. As one New England primary school principal wisely remarked, "The drop-out problem starts right down there in kindergarten and first grade, with children whose parents start them in school before they are ready. They fail early, come to hate school and drop out as soon as the opportunity presents itself."

Or, as a West Virginia educator sensibly commented, "We are all too ready, in our schools, to force children to respond to learning stimuli before their neuromuscular systems are capable of making correct responses. This early forcing has its beginning in our very first teachings of the language arts—listening, speaking, reading and writing. *No child sets out in life to be a failure, a retardee, a drop-out or a juvenile delinquent.* He learns to be one. He learns to be one by being literally forced to become one because of his inability to adjust himself to the learning stimuli presented to him in school."

Parents, it is to a large extent up to you to try to prevent your own boy or girl from becoming a drop-out, an underachiever or any other kind of school failure. It is our hope that the advice and information in this present book may help a good many of you to give your children the help they need to insure a successful school career.

# Chapter 2

## DON'T START HIM IN

## TOO YOUNG

"WHEN children have to repeat in my school, I can almost predict which ones it will be, even before the teachers turn in their reports," a New England primary school principal told us recently.

"It will be mostly boys. And nearly every one of them will be a November or December or January birthday boy who started first grade before he was six."

This may seem like an awfully flat statement. But we ourselves could say the same thing. There are exceptions to any rule, but this principal has found, as we have, that it's an unusual boy who is ready for first grade before he is fully six.

In fact, our own figures, as well as those arrived at by many other educators throughout the country, agree that the older children are when they start school, the better they tend to do. If primary children in the "high" and in the "low" groups of any given grade are divided into the older pupils whose birthdays fall before June (making them six years and three months or older before they start first grade) and those whose birthdays fall on or after July first (making them six years and two months or younger when starting first grade), the majority of those on the older side are found to be in the high groups, those on the younger side in low groups. There are many exceptions, of course, but the general

10

rule holds up that the child who is on the older side has the better chance of doing well in school.

In an ideal school setup, *every* child would be examined by means of a careful behavior, or school readiness, examination before the time of school entrance. Such an examination would indicate whether or not he is ready for the work of the grade to which his legal age assigns him.

However, at the present time this is not always possible, and so the majority of schools continue to enter children on the basis of their chronological age. This age requirement varies a very great deal from state to state, and seems often to depend more on legislative whim than on anything that common sense or experience might suggest.

Fortunately, there is now in evidence a strong tendency to move the cut-off date increasingly toward September first, but there are many glaring exceptions. Thus, in the state of Pennsylvania, at this writing, a child can enter kindergarten in September if he is going to be five in the *following* January. Our own city of New Haven, Connecticut, has a similar rule. To enter kindergarten a child needs only to have his fifth birthday before the first of the following February, which means that a child not yet four years and eight months can begin kindergarten. A child only five years and eight months can start first grade.

The fact that children can, in many communities, enter school when they are so very young results, quite naturally, in many of them starting in long before they are ready. Furthermore, because children vary so tremendously, one from the other, in their level of maturity at any given age, it turns out in actual practice that even many of those who are full six-year-olds are not yet ready for the work of first grade.

All of this has caused many people, ourselves included, to look with considerable suspicion on age as the criterion for deciding when a child will be ready to go to school.

And yet, in spite of tremendous individual differences, children are alike enough so that if the legal entrance age were high enough, it would in the majority of cases probably do the trick, assuming that individual readiness examinations could not be given.

The trouble with the age usually set (five for kindergarten, six for first grade) is that, as these grades are taught now in most schools, though the upper 25 or 50 percent of the children of this age *may* by able to do the work in question, the bottom 50 percent or even more often are not ready, and thus flounder hopelessly.

Thus unless widespread and far-reaching changes in curriculum can be arranged in most of our schools, it might be safer and more satisfactory if we thought of having children closer to five-and-a-half than to five years of age when they started kindergarten, closer to six-and-a-half than to six when they started first grade.

However it may actually not be necessary to go quite so far. The majority of parents and teachers are aware of the fact that in general girls develop, in the early years of life, considerably more rapidly than do boys. There are of course exceptions—late developing girls, early developing boys.

Most everybody knows about this discrepancy in behavior level and rate of development of the two sexes, but almost nobody does anything practical about it. It would be our recommendation, if individual behavior examinations cannot be given to every child at the time he enters either kindergarten or first grade, that girls be fully five before they start kindergarten, fully six before starting first grade. We prefer boys to be fully five-and-a-half for kindergarten, fully six-and-a-half for first grade.

We'll let several mothers of fall boys (and the mother of one fall girl) give you their views on the dangers of starting such children too soon:

I truly wish that *every* mother in all of America, with children under six years of age, woud *drop everything* and read and reread one of your columns which points out that not all children are ready for first grade just because they happen to be six years of age. And that very few of those not yet six are ready, no matter how bright you may consider them.

All children born in the months of October, November and December should *not* be registered in the September preceding their sixth birthday, even though you may be *waiting* most anxiously for your child to start school, and even though you think and know that your child is exceptionally brilliant. Please remember one thing—that if you keep him home and suffer through one more year with him, you will be amply repaid in the years to come. Your dividends will be great— very great. Give up just *one more year*—please listen, just one more year. How happy you will be later on!

And here's another mother with the same story:

I was absolutely thrilled when my two December birthday sons just made registration by five and six weeks. I thought it was the best thing that ever happened to me. I did not then realize how unlucky I was. My two boys were always nine and ten months younger than everyone else in their grades. They kept up, but were by no means outstanding. I know now that if they had been one year below their present grades, both boys would have been more anxious to study and learn.

Today I am a *worrying* mother, hoping that my sons will complete college in spite of their earlier mediocre performance in school. All these years of anxiety simply because I never understood what one more year at home could have done for my children and for me. I write this hoping and praying that some other mothers, somewhere, will learn from my own sad experience.

A *Canadian* mother has this to say:

My son Clifford was a December boy, five years and nine months old when he started first grade. Although I instinctively felt he was immature, and was in full agreement with your views, nevertheless I sent him to school.

The experiment lasted two weeks. The change in him, for the worse, was so striking you wouldn't believe it. From the happy little boy he had been, he became a whining, tired, demanding youngster. He was physically exhausted and though I sent him to bed earlier, he was still too tired to get up in the morning.

So Cliff and I talked it over and decided we needed more time for our walks, and that school would be more fun next year. He was a little reluctant at first, but I let him take his new lunch pail outdoors and eat in the sunshine, and now he and I both feel better about the whole thing. I know I made the right decision.

This mother instinctively felt that her son was immature, or just too young, but, and we sympathize, until the whole school structure changes and everybody respects the notion of readiness, it *is* hard to go against everybody and keep a child out when the school and the law say he is ready to start. So, she made a mistake. Fortunately she was one of the wise ones who realized her mistake early. And acted upon that recognition!

*And this from an Iowa mother:*

It is our wish to have our son retained in fourth grade this coming year. We feel he is lost, trying to compete with children who are one and even two years older. Since he is a quiet, reserved boy, with little self-confidence, we feel that being with children his own age or younger will be to his advantage.

We were hoping he would have been kept back in kindergarten. Likewise in first, second and third grade. Nobody would listen. Now we feel that the adjustment *must* be made. The longer it is put off, the harder it will be on him. The work is increasingly hard for him every year.

We feel that being in fourth grade again next year will bolster his morale, as he will catch on to the studies more easily than the others and will feel he is more capable. We feel he has the ability to make good grades and want him given the chance.

What can we say? "We were hoping he would have been kept back in kindergarten and first and second and third grade," say these perceptive parents and thousands like them. "Now [they concluded] the adjustment must be made." But so late!

Don't let this letter from a parent, sent to us by a Wisconsin educator, be your child's story:

Please urge parents of children, but especially of boys, born after August to "wait a year" before enrolling them in kindergarten. Urge teachers to be more selective in all students they promote to first grade. Don't allow a child to get as far as fourth grade before waiting to hold him back. Impress on teachers that it is not a black mark against them if all their pupils are not promoted. We deeply appreciate the cooperation and guidance of our son's teacher and principal when we decided to hold him back after he completed—if you can call it completing—third grade.

This story obviously has a happy ending and contains, in a short space, a good deal of excellent advice.

*Another Iowa mother tells us:*

My daughter Tracy is eight years old and nearly through third grade. She didn't do well in first grade but at the end of the year the teacher said she would catch up. Second grade wasn't much better, but that teacher said the same thing.

Now Tracy is no better in third grade. The teacher says the reason for her low grades is that she doesn't try. She says Tracy could do better if she would only put her mind to it. Says she doesn't use her time wisely, doesn't follow directions, doesn't finish her work.

Tracy is the youngest in her class. Most others are nine or will be soon. But the teacher says age doesn't make that much difference since Tracy is bright. She started kindergarten before she was five and I know now it was a mistake. Do you think I should insist that she repeat third grade?

This teacher unfortunately seems to have mastered *all* the untrue clichés which the unknowing muster in defense of overplacement. They are all here: "She's not quite ready now but she'll catch up"; "she could do better if she would"; "Age doesn't matter; it's the intelligence that counts."

To answer the mother's question: Yes, you *should* insist that Tracy repeat third grade. But preferably with a different teacher.

# *Chapter 3*

## PARENTS WARN, "GO SLOWLY"

THERE are two ways of being unready for the work of a given grade. The first and most obvious way is to be too young in birthday age. The second and more dangerous way (because it is harder to spot) is to be too *immature,* or too young in behavior even though theoretically old enough in years. A six-year-old who behaves like a five-year-old would be considered immature. Though the laws of many state indicate that a child just under six years of age (and in some states five-and-a-half years old) is legally ready to start first grade, we find that in many instances such a child is too young in his behavior and thus not ready.

It is important for parents to realize that there is nothing adverse intended by the term immature. A mother recently told us that she thought the teacher was "mean" to say this about her son. It is no meaner to say of a child that he is immature than to say that he is below average height for his age, or that he is nearsighted.

Immaturity is not bad. And it does not imply, as some believe, that a child is not intelligent. Level of intelligence and level of maturity are two separate variables, so that it is quite possible for a child to be superior *but* immature. In fact, "superior-immature" is a term we use to describe the bright but babyish child, who confuses parents and teachers by being bright, and perhaps able to read, and yet is so immature in general ways that the school or the child specialist may rule him not ready for first grade.

16

Immaturity means merely that a child is behind the average for his age in the way his behavior, or his body, is developing. Immaturity is a warning that a child is growing a little more slowly than the average and thus needs a little extra time to do his growing.

Parents themselves have turned out to be our best press agents in our effort to help people realize that not all children are ready to start school at the age which the law prescribes.

The idea that hard work and sincere effort are not enough to guarantee successful school performance in a normally bright child *of legal school age* who is not emotionally disturbed, brain-damaged or handicapped in any major way, is new to many. In fact it is only recently that we ourselves have fully realized that adequate age and intelligence and emotional stability (plus a good home background and a good school with good teaching) are not necessarily enough to guarantee superior or even adequate school performance.

The factor which looms with increasing importance as our knowledge about children in school increases is the factor of maturity. The infant, no matter how rich the environment and how enthusiastic the efforts of his parents, doesn't walk, doesn't talk, until his entire organism is ready. Similarly, the ordinary child is not able to do a good job with the demands of kindergarten or first grade (or whatever the grade may be) until he has matured to a certain point.

Hard work is not enough. Conscientious effort and a willingness to try and to conform to parents' and teachers' demands and requirements are not enough. The child must be ready for *all* the demands of a grade (not just the academic demands) before we can anticipate success.

This chapter reports the experiences of a dozen parents from Maine to Oregon as they tell about their unready children. Some of these parents were smart enough, or fortunate enough, to be able to correct or prevent that too early start or that continued overplacement, often in the face of considerable resistance. Others failed to do so and their failure became their children's failure. But the theme of all is the same—an unready child struggling with the demands of a grade he wasn't ready for.

If the theme of these letters seems repetitive, all the better, from our point of view. We look forward to the day when it will be a universal theme. Then all parents and teachers will be as quick as we ourselves have become to spot, and to do something about, that child who is not ready for his grade.

This letter is from a Philadelphia mother:

My son, Randy, age five-and-a-half, started kindergarten this September. For a few days he did well, ate a full breakfast and seemed happy to be going to school. Then he started being sick to his stomach every morning and crying, but finally agreeing to go.

Now things are worse. He won't dress himself and he won't let me dress him. I have to hold, force and hit to get him to hold still so I can get his clothes on. I have to carry him down the stairs or pull and threaten.

My pediatrician says to keep forcing him to go to school and he will overcome his fear and refusal If not for this doctor's stern advice to make him go, I would take him out of kindergarten now and wait another year.

What I want to know—is it correct for me to continue forcing Randy to go to school?

As often happens, the bad effects of a too early start in school showed up at home rather than at school. *Any very marked change for the worse in a kindergarten or first-grade child's disposition or home behavior, especially when the child is a boy and a bit on the young side, should alert a mother to the possibility that her child is not ready for that particular school experience.*

In Randy's case things are complicated by the advice of a stern and unsympathetic physician. Fortunately, not many doctors are so unknowing.

This letter is from a mother from Maine:

A week after I wrote you, and even before receiving your reply, we took Jessie out of school. Now we plan to start her in kindergarten, again, next fall. This we did in the face of disagreement from the school and others. The details I'll skip but I will say this. We know in our hearts that we have done the right thing, and what others say doesn't count.

We had been so sure that Jessie would be ready for school. She talked about it and looked forward to it, but she sure was unready. And such an improvement already! She spends many happy hours with me or playing by herself. She still throws a tantrum now and then but how much more relaxed and happy this little girl is.

In a way it's good that your letter was late. I was waiting for someone to tell me what to do. As it was I had to find the answers for myself, but your letter strengthens and confirms my thoughts on this matter. You people are making tremendous strides in bringing us out of the dark ages into a better understanding of our children and ourselves.

Jessie's story illustrates the fact that though a child's enthusiasm about starting school can be a good sign, it is not always a guarantee of readiness.

This mother's phrase "dark ages" may seem an exaggeration, but fifty or a hundred years from now people will, we believe, look back and our present methods will seem to warrant this description.

Here is a letter from a New York mother:

May I tell you about our daughter Lisa, now nine, who did not seem ready for kindergarten at the age of five. Though the school urged us to start her, both her father and I were not satisfied that she was ready, and after weighing all the angles we decided that she should wait another year.

We were visited by the Child Guidance teacher and the nurse. They told us we were doing wrong in not insisting that she attend. Our answer was that we had decided she was not ready. She did start when she was six—and from the beginning has had a wonderful attitude toward her teachers and toward everything connected with school. She is 100 percent happy and adjusted and gets above-average grades in all her classes.

We know without a doubt that many children are forced to start school too soon. This affects their nerves and general health all through their school lives. We find that our daughter is ready for everything she is presented at school and that she derives to the full extent the full meaning and value of all she is taught. This would not have been true had we insisted that she start school at five.

The school nurse made it a point to speak to me and admit that we did exactly the right thing in having Lisa wait the extra year. We parents are fully responsible for our little ones, far beyond the point of feeding and clothing them. Each one is an individual and their parents should recognize their readiness, or unreadiness, for the demands of life.

Please keep up your good work and open all the parents' eyes— wide.

This good letter from a Salt Lake City mother speaks for itself and needs little further comment:

My own experience this past two years is certain proof that parents need to know how to handle the situation when they have an immature youngster.

My daughter Sally turned five the last part of June so she was, supposedly, of the right age to enter kindergarten in September. I was sure she wasn't ready, but each time I mentioned this to friends or relatives they all said, "Oh, she'll get along fine once she gets going."

Well, she never did get along fine, either in kindergarten, first grade or second grade. And she knew it. We had her tutored summers, but this only made her summers miserable.

Near the end of second grade she informed me that she had decided to go to second grade again. She didn't know the work and couldn't go on to third until she could do second.

This she did. The teacher told the other children that repeating second grade was Sally's own decision. The teacher and I were both so proud of the dear child, that she herself recognized what WE should have known. However, she would have been spared three years of school she wasn't ready for, and I would have been spared the worry and wondering and the constant pushing, had we all had sense enough to let her stay out of school another year as we should have done.

This story may surprise readers, but this child is by no means unique. We have heard of numerous other children, though seldom one so young, who were smart enough to recognize their own unreadiness for the grade in which Fate had placed them. We predict that a girl with so much insight, and the ability to act on that insight, will go far.

Here is a letter from another New York mother:

Our son Danny is starting third grade this fall. Every year we try to get him held back and every year the school refuses, saying that he is old enough to do the work and also that there would be a stigma to being held back and that children thrive on difficulties.

Danny seems to be one of those boys you describe as superior-immature, bright but very, very young-acting for his age. His reactions to school have been all those you describe as symptoms of possible unreadiness: dawdling, objecting and sick to his stomach in the morning. In school, inattention, daydreaming, not concentrating, not doing his work and bothering the other children. At home he is tired, irritable, unhappy.

The school has dealt with this by isolating him, sending him to the principal's office, scolding, smacking and even pulling his hair. None of these methods accomplishes anything.

We fear that this problem is affecting not only his adjustment to school but his home life and physical health as well. His behavior at home during the school year is very rebellious; when school is out, his behavior is very much improved. Is there anything we can do to make the school let Danny repeat?

This mother is one of the all too many whose child is suffering the clear effect of being overplaced. So far as we know a parent has a "right" to insist that his child be retained. (Though not the opposite—it is the school which should determine any extra promotion.) We look forward to the day when problems like this mother's will no longer exist. Even though today there are many schools which will not comply with such a request, there are many which would welcome this mother's realistic evaluation of her son's consistent immaturity.

A letter from a Wisconsin father:

All parents should keep in mind that precocity does not reveal maturity level. Our son was bright but immature physically and emotionally for his grade level. Thanks to the school's interest we finally, when he got to fourth grade, made the decision which should have been made three years earlier. His changed behavior, both at home and school, shows us that we made the right decision.

Better late than never. Some parents fear that because they failed to keep their child back in kindergarten or first grade, it is then too late to make the needed adjustment. It's true that each year of overplacement compounds a child's confusion, but just because you made a mistake in the past is no reason to go on making that same mistake.

The following letter is from a West Virginia mother:

I want to thank you for the immeasurable help you have given me through the years. One specific example is your help with my son Dale. He just finished eighth grade at the head of his class and I can thank you for that.

It is because of your countless newspaper articles about boys starting first grade too soon that I had the support I needed to keep Dale in kindergarten an extra year. This was not easy. My friends, my husband, the teachers and principal all assured me that he would be fine to go ahead to first grade. But I knew better. He was immature in so many ways.

It is gratifying to realize that Dale knows, too, what an advantage he has had over other boys in his class, socially as well as intellectually, by being on the older side. It is very discouraging to see how slow educators are to realize the importance of this.

It hurts me to see so many little boys failing in school simply because they are not ready. Just in our neighborhood I can count nine who have finally had to repeat a year, and there are many others who are on the brink. The really sad thing about this is that in many cases these boys dislike school always because they've had a bad start. It is so unnecessary, and I hope you will keep pounding away at parents and educators.

This mother's story, unlike most in this chapter, has both a happy beginning and a happy ending. We hope to see a time when this boy's experience will be the rule rather than the exception.

A mother from Oregon wrote the following letter:

Too bad it took so long to find out what some people already knew twenty years ago—that children cannot go any faster in school than their own growth rate permits. But you can't get teachers to see it. Our seventeen-year-old daughter is one of those who is paying the price today because she was not ready for second grade but was put there anyway.

It's heartbreaking to see children struggling along over their heads and no way to rescue them. I talked with the teacher and begged her to let Sophy repeat first grade. But NO. She had to be promoted. Same thing in second grade and third. I just *begged* to have her kept back. But all they would say was that she was a dear little girl and got along well with everyone.

Now Sophy has grown to hate school. The results of your studies will perhaps make teachers see things in a different light. I have always felt that learning and study should be a happy experience for the child and not a burden.

Sophy is just one of the all too many "too much too soon" children. May the time come when her experience will be the glaring exception rather than an everyday occurrence.

Even stronger than the voices of parents who know that their children were overplaced and who have seen for themselves the often almost miraculous change which occurs when an adjustment is made, are the voices of those adults who started school too early and went through school too fast. All too many end up shy and lacking in self-confidence.

Thus here's the story of a woman, now grown, who had the great misfortune of being pushed through school too fast, just because she was bright. She tells us:

Congratulations on your advice to mothers not to skip their children simply because they seem bright. Keep on telling them NOT to skip their boys and girls no matter how bright they are. I can assure you from my own experience that skipping leads straight to disaster.

I was skipped and skipped again. Started fifth grade when I was eight; finished college when I was nineteen. No trouble about grades— studies were easy for me. But to this day I must count on my fingers.

And how lonely I was. I was always too immature, both physically and psychically, for the group I was with. Many of my social and personal, and even professional, failures in adult life I lay to the fact that I went too fast, much too fast, all the way through school.

There is nobody more appreciative of the vital importance of starting school at the "right" time and proceeding at a comfortable and reasonable pace, nobody who feels more strongly about the misery, unhappiness and failure that incorrect placement can cause, then the adult who has traveled the unhappy road of over-placement himself.

# Chapter 4

## DON'T BE AFRAID TO REPEAT

IF it turns out that you *did* start your child in school too early, and if it turns out that he is not capable of doing the work of the grade to which age assigned him, should you keep him back and have him repeat a grade? Will such a child as a repeater be able to do the work expected of the children in his room, become happy and well adjusted, relaxed and confident as well as a more effective student, once he is correctly placed? Or will what some people anticipate as the emotional damage which repeating causes more than balance the good which may come of repeating?

We're going to let a handful of typical mothers speak for themselves. (This handful could be multiplied almost infinitely if space permitted, and we can truthfully say that we have never personally heard of an instance in which repeating was emotionally harmful to anybody.)

Dear Doctors:

I want to corroborate your contention that our son Bobby (thirteen years old last month) was definitely overplaced in school. And that all his unhappiness and inability to adjust to junior high school would be wiped away if only we would let him repeat seventh grade this year.

Frankly, I was very skeptical that what appeared deep trouble in him could be so easily corrected. Well, I was wrong and you were 100 percent right. You would not recognize Bob as the same boy this year. This fall we started him in seventh instead of eighth. He was willing. And he is now one happy, outgoing child—good marks, friends, a member of the school orchestra and apparently liked by his classmates.

24

In short, many many thanks to you and many bouquets for your advice and insight. And boos to those specialists who were sure that Bobby needed psychotherapy. Our whole family is relaxed and happy at his newfound happiness.

Dear Doctors:

I just had to write to tell you about the firm stand I took when our school refused to hold back our nine-year-old son, Paul. First grade was a struggle for Paul and so were second, third and fourth. But they said he could do the work if only he weren't so lazy.

Finally they promoted him to fifth grade and it was then I took my stand. I was late but firm. In fact, I was a *rock* to all the tears, arguments and pressures from every side. I was determined that this farce was not going to continue any longer.

Now more time has gone by. Paul is in the grade he belongs in and we are all happy about the whole thing. My only regret is that I didn't pull him right out of first grade when the trouble started and keep him home till he was seven and really ready.

Dear Doctors:

I must tell you of the fight, a real fight, I had to have my daughter Josie repeat first grade. Josie has a September birthday and just made their first-grade entrance age. I had qualms about this but registered her anyway. The third week of school she came home crying. Seems the teacher took her on her lap and sang "Rockabye Baby" to her in front of the class because she couldn't stop talking.

I guess you know who was at that school next day! The teacher and I went the rounds until the holidays were over, then I went over her head to the principal and demanded that Josie be put back in kinder-garten *where her stupid mother should have put her in the first place*.

We had a three-way conference that turned out one way—*mine!* The teacher kept saying, "But I can *make* Josie learn the work!"

Needless to say, Josie went to kindergarten for the rest of the year and loved it. And went sailing through the grades which followed. She is an excellent reader today and doesn't mind at all that she is older than many in her class.

Dear Doctors:

As the mother of a child who was finally allowed to stay back, I can't thank you enough for your advice that "the emotional harm of repeating never measures up to the total harm of being in a grade where you don't belong."

Basically I have never been a fighter and couldn't stand up to the school authorities. My one ray of hope was the new school psychologist who tested my third-grade son George and found him to be superior but reading only at a second-grade level. It was only because of his recommendation that George was allowed to repeat second grade.

He accepted the news well enough at first, but the day before school started brought a deluge of tears, self-pity and rebellion. I sat in the rocking chair for an hour with my tall eight-year-old son, comforting him but holding fast to an irrevocable decision.

Finally I took him to a friend's house. This boy was in second grade and as we left I said jokingly, "Joe, if George forgets who he is tomorrow, you tell the teacher for him." The boys laughed, but it turned the trick! George had been afraid to walk into the room alone and introduce himself.

From that day on he never had any trouble. The other students were kind and he soon found himself near the top of the class instead of at the bottom. An unexpected bonus from my campaign is that now five children are repeating kindergarten at our school for the very first time.

A North Carolina mother reports the almost instant success of having her son stay back a grade:

We were so happy and grateful to read your newspaper column in which you warned about the dangers of overplacement. It helped my husband and me to make what we believe to be one of the most important decisions we have ever made concerning our oldest son.

Don is eleven years old, rather small for his age and has always been both aggressive and shy. It's hard to understand this kind of child and hard to help him. School has always, for him, been a place where he did not fit and didn't know why.

He was to go into sixth grade this past September, and we knew full well that he would just be getting in deeper and deeper. How to help him? We prayed for an answer. Then in August we read your column. *It hit us like a ton of bricks.* Of course! This was where the problem lay. Don was really overplaced in school. Not academically, but on the social behavior level, straining to the breaking point to perform beyond his degree of maturity. *How had we been so blind?* I think we made the mistake because his birthday was May 7 and we had taken it for granted that he was old enough.

So we made our decision, then secured the principal's cooperation, then our son's. We won't pretend that it was entirely easy. But little did we expect to see the immediate results which came forth. After the initial adjustment had been made our child began to go about the house *singing!* It was as though a heavy weight had been lifted from his shoulders.

We are more and more certain as the weeks of school slip by that this is going to be a great school year for our son. But more than that, a great year to be alive. How much easier to show your love to a child who is on the march at his own pace than to one who is floundering and drowning before your very eyes and you don't know how to save him.

Here's what a California clergyman has to say on the same subject:

I am writing in regard to my son Kenneth, who was replaced from the sixth to the fifth grade last January. At that time, Kenneth was manifesting many of the symptoms of an overplaced child: rebellious behavior, refusal to do his homework, crying, etc. I must confess that I was rather doubtful about having him replaced—possibly some of my own feelings of pride were involved.

During the following months we became aware of a change taking place in Kenneth. Fewer and fewer of the above-mentioned symptoms and more desire on his part to accept himself. He was quite proud that he could do the work so well. On the playground, now, he is asked to take part. His handwriting has improved, his attitude has improved and he now seems to feel adequate for the role expected of him.

All in all it is like living with a new son, and we must give credit where it is due. . . . We do hope that this concept of recognizing overplacement when it is present can spread to other schools, for it has made a great difference in the inner structure of our family. We feel a great debt to the school's handling of the problem and deep regret that other school systems do not pay more attention to the important matter of corrected grade placement.

These letters are from typical parents, and they could be from you, if you have the good fortune to be one of the hundreds of thousands of parents in this country whose children have the privilege of repeating when repeating is indicated. What, on the other hand, would your story be if you know you should keep your child back, but don't? Let still another mother speak for you:

Dear Doctors:

My oldest son, Derrick, started first grade when he was several months short of six years old. I knew almost at once that the work was too hard for him but nobody would ever listen to me. They all insisted that he could do the work if he would only apply himself.

Years went by, with me ineffectively complaining to the school but not really having the necessary stamina to take a strong stand.

Result? Years of crying and fussing, and constant pressure at school, of urging and tutoring at home. The accumulated years of constant struggle, inadequacy, frustration and discouragement finally caught up with Derrick in his junior and senior high school years.

Here his social immaturity combined with monumental self-doubt began to show itself in deep-seated and morbid anxieties. He was and still is very self-depreciating and miserable and is now taking professional psychiatric counseling in an effort to re-establish his perspective and self-appreciation.

Here was a youngster of better-than-average intelligence, creative and with a good environment and (we think) conscientious parents, and with a driving desire to measure up to what was expected of him and to his own demanding ideal, crushed by twelve school years of unequal struggle.

I don't blame anyone but myself for not having had the courage to stand up for what I knew was best, instead of accepting the "professional wisdom and reassurance" of school authorities.

Well if it's all so wonderful, readers may ask, why doesn't every mother keep her child back as soon as she recognizes that he is overplaced?

One reason—pride. Even a very perceptive parent may initially, under present conditions (and until everybody comes to recognize the importance of every child being in the grade to which his behavior age and general ability and maturity level assign him), have a feeling that her child is *failing* if he can't keep up with the grade he started in.

Such pride is false pride and such logic is incorrect. Unless some careful check is made on maturity level, you don't really know that your child should be in this grade which is turning out to be too much for him.

Some parents *do* recognize overplacement and *do* try to have a child held back, but meet with resistance on the part of the school. We're glad to say that, increasingly, schools are recognizing the value of having a child repeat when behavior or achievement tests show the need of repeating.

Probably the main reason, however, that parents, teachers, principals and school psychologists hesitate about having a child repeat, or even firmly oppose repeating, is the widely held but incorrect notion that to have a child repeat a grade will harm him emotionally.

Many sincere people genuinely believe that it *will* harm a child emotionally if he is required to repeat. Unfortunately at this time no clear research results are available which prove or disprove the theory that a child suffers psychic damage by being kept back.

Certainly in most cases, unless a child is unusually rational, or his parents are able to do a remarkably good job in presenting the notion to him in the first place, one must expect a few tears and tantrums, a few general threats of leaving home (or the country) and a general, initial, feeling that he has failed, once it has been decided that he must repeat.

With most children, tears are replaced more quickly than you might expect by smiles and cheerful comments that "Now I'm one of the smartest," "Now I can lick any guy in the room," "School is fun now," "I knew I couldn't do it and I wondered when they'd find it out," "I'm glad they put me back to first grade because I *love* space." (The first-graders were doing a project on space.) In fact the tears, if any, may be tears of happiness as in the case of the little boy who cried when the principal told him he was going back to first grade.

"Why are you crying, Billy?" asked the principal.

"Because I'm so glad," was Billy's reply.

Some children are of course more vulnerable than others; some bounce back more quickly than do others. Each child is different. But in most cases, once initial unhappy emotions have died down, the child's long-term reaction to the fact of repeating rests squarely on the parents' shoulders. If you genuinely feel that this is the right move to make, if you truly realize that it is the child's too early placement that is at fault and not the child, if you sincerely approve of having him in the lower grade where he can fit and function effectively, he will in all probability accept your verdict that this was a good thing to do.

His new success in doing the work in a grade for which his ability and maturity level suit him will do the rest.

At least try this simple remedy first before you spend hours and dollars on tutoring, remedial reading, summertime instruction or psychotherapy. Try the simple and more natural remedy first. Don't be like the parents who got around to letting their daughter repeat a grade only after she had had nine months of psychotherapy, an experience which was harrowing for everyone including the therapist, who finally gave up. This father's comment to us was, "Six weeks of being in the right grade have done more for Hilda than nine months of psychotherapy."

One final thought on this subject of repeating—how far should you go with it? If a child has repeated once and it hasn't done the trick, would there be any advantage to having him repeat again? Yes, in some cases there would. If a slow-maturing boy has been started in first grade when he was, say, just under six years of age, when in actual fact he wasn't going to be ready for first-grade work till he was eight (which can happen with a normal but slow-developing boy), a second repetition might be in order.

Beyond that, that is if a child has been repeated twice and it hasn't done the trick, we would consider that he was clearly not suited for the work of a regular type of classroom and might in all likelihood need some special type of schooling.

Not every child who repeats will then perform his school work effectively. This is to be expected. Repeating a grade is no magic formula which will cure everything. But if a child is required to repeat because his behavior is not up to the work of the grade, if he is only one grade ahead of the grade he belongs in and there are no other major complicating factors, experience shows (at least our experience shows) that *almost without exception the child's performance at school is conspicuously improved.*

However, children are repeated for many other reasons. Some fail in school because of low intelligence, some because of serious personality problems. Some children do not belong in the regular type of classroom at *any* grade level.

Repeating a grade will not give a child the intelligence he may seriously lack. It will not, of itself, provide emotional stability in the emotionally unstable child. It *can* lighten the load but still cannot guarantee success for the child who belongs in a special classroom.

But if a child's poor response to school in a grade to which age has assigned him is caused chiefly by immaturity and unreadiness for that grade, repeating will in most cases work wonders.

## A Proposed Alternative to Repeating

There is a new kind of primary school setup now being tried rather extensively in this country which aims to prevent the necessity of having any child repeat. This method is called the ungraded primary.

In this so-called ungraded primary the first three "grades" are ungraded, and children proceed at supposedly their own pace for three or if necessary four years before they finally are presumed ready to enter the usual formal fourth grade. This arrangement would presumably remove any necessity of anybody repeating a grade, since there are no grades to begin with, and no child is required to proceed at any more than his own comfortable pace.

We feel very positive and friendly toward the ungraded primary idea, because its supporters are aiming very much at the same goal we ourselves are trying to reach—every child in a learning situation which is suited to *him*.

Exponents of the ungraded primary recognize exactly the same problem and difficulties in the present educational setup which we do. That is, they emphasize the fact that not all children are ready for any given grade at some arbitrary age. They respect the fact that not all children develop at the same rate as do others, even once started. And they recognize that many children may be good in one subject, poor in another.

In actual practice, ungraded primaries vary tremendously as

they are carried out in different communities. Some do seem to be carrying out their aims very effectively. In many, however, the notion has not turned out too well in actual practice. Some have had good luck with their method of having, in the first three years, twelve or twenty or even thirty-two reading levels and then letting each child progress through these at his own pace. However, this method has two drawbacks. For many children, performance in reading may be way ahead of or way behind other subjects. Thus reading level alone makes a poor basis for grouping.

More than that, many leaders in the ungraded primary movement consider the use of reading levels to be "too stratified." They recommend instead what are called "overlapping classroom habitats,"* with at least a three-year span of abilities in each classroom. Books would be given out on an almost individual basis—four of this book, five of that, eight of that.

Most discouraging is the conclusion of experts on this type of program that "educators planning to develop non-graded plans *are not helped much* by visits to schools calling themselves ungraded because such ungraded schools as we now have tend to slip back into old ways of teaching, grouping and thinking."

Our personal impression is that "old ways" may not be so bad at that. Admittedly the whole notion of ungraded primary has done much good in that it has served to break up the old lock-step idea that every child at six must start first grade and that everybody must proceed at exactly the same rate.

What we would prefer, however, would be to break up the lock-step and *then* place each child not in the supposedly boundless freedom of an ungraded primary, but rather in the special grade or group in which he really belongs. And we personally prefer to give the group its proper name. Labels are not necessarily invidious. And Goodlad himself has commented recently in public lecture that it might be better to keep the grade labels and teach

---

* For the most up-to-date book available on ungraded schools see Goodlad and Anderson, *The Nongraded Elementary School* (Harcourt, Brace, 1963).

flexibly rather than to give up grade labels and then teach in a rigid way.

Thus there is much that is good which can be said about the whole notion of the ungraded primary, but it has not always worked out too well in actual practice. And we ourselves prefer to retain the grade notion, to take the greatest of pains to see that no child starts school before he is fully ready and to have him repeat should it turn out that he is not up to the work of the grade in which he finds himself.

## Chapter 5

## TEACHERS AND PRINCIPALS

## ARE ON YOUR SIDE

"THOSE teachers! I've been trying for five years to get my son held back but it's impossible. It's been just fight, fight, fight, and I get nowhere."

Many of you parents have indeed found that it's an uphill struggle to get the school to recognize the fact that your son or daughter may need to go more slowly.

Would it surprise you to know that many teachers feel the same way about "the parents" as you may about "the teacher"? Many and many an elementary school teacher has complained to us, "There are half a dozen children in my room who really don't belong there. But it's a hopeless fight trying to get their parents to accept the fact."

Readers, may we assure you—it isn't just "the teachers" or "the parents" who fail to recognize, even when the facts speak starkly for themselves, that a boy or girl is overplaced.

There are many parents, and many teachers, many psychologists, school administrators and guidance people who are fully aware of the dangers of overplacement; fully able to recognize those individual cases where a child needs to go more slowly.

The problem is that, in this instance, it takes three to tango . . . or perhaps more properly speaking, four. Mother, father, teacher

34

and principal, *all four* more or less have to agree. And may we digress here to say just a word about fathers?

It's an all too common story that a mother is able to recognize and act on her child's need to go more slowly in school, but it tends to be the father who holds out and insists that his son is not going to go more slowly and not going to repeat. Then, all too often, the mother has to fight her husband *and* the school and it's just too much and she gives up.

This reaction on the part of fathers is by no means entirely unreasonable or hard to understand. Fathers are for the most part even more ambitious for their children than are mothers. Mothers, ambitious or not, being at home with their children more than fathers are, are more able to make a correct evaluation of real abilities. They, more than the fathers, observe and sense a child's unhappiness when he is pushed too hard. Most are willing to compromise on their aims and ambitions in favor of having their child comfortable and happy.

Mothers, too, being so constantly with the child from infancy onward, if they are at all realistic, do have the opportunity, and the need, to come to grips with immaturity when it is present. It is the father who in the preschool years commands, "It's time now that he does so and so." Mothers know that time or not, some children are not, no matter what father says, at some given age able to stay dry, count to ten or do the work of first grade.

Mother's pride seems as a rule less involved than is father's in having a child who is at the top of his class, and in the usual class for his age.

All of this is involved in the refusal of many a father to listen to the very notion that his child be held back in school. However, little by little, fathers are beginning to accept the fact, which so many mothers in this country have already come to terms with, that some children do need to go more slowly than others and that not all six-year-olds are equally mature and ready for the first grade.

Some fathers do this on the basis of their own, remembered,

school experiences. The father who himself was as a child in the category which we label as "superior-immature" (that is intellectually superior but behaviorally immature) is often the one who most quickly and easily accepts the notion that his son, too, may be better off if allowed to proceed a little more slowly through school.

Now, emerging from our parenthesis, let's return to the subject of teachers and school administrators and their attitude toward having children go more slowly and repeat when necessary.

We truly can assure you that if you as a parent have had a bad experience with some teacher or teachers who refused to let your child repeat, that an equally large number of teachers have had a similarly bad time with parents. That is, we'd like to assure you that there is not a large body made up of *all the teachers* just standing there adamant, unaware of the fact that many children are going too fast and do need to repeat, and unwilling to let them do so.

Knowing this may make you feel better about the whole thing. While it may not solve your own immediate problem, it will at least keep you from thinking, as some do, that you parents are all lined up on one side and the teachers all lined up on the other side, against you.

See for yourselves what a handful of teachers (typical of hundreds of others we know) have to say on the subject:

A California teacher comments:

I agree absolutely with you that many children need to go more slowly in school. Having had almost thirty years' experience teaching, I have seen this over and over, parents too eager to push their children along in school. If we continue this way we will develop a generation of psychological misfits. What can we as teachers do about it? If only parents could appreciate the tortures and torment these little ones suffer when they are in a grade they just are not ready for.

Another teacher tells us about a little boy named Erwin, who, she says is

a perfectly average, quiet, pleasant, but very immature little boy who should have started first grade a year later than he did. He seems to live in apprehension lest he disappoint his mother, who is tense and dynamic and tends to force issues at Erwin's expense.

We here at school feel she is creating a problem where none need exist. We have recommended retention each year, but the very thought is so upsetting to Erwin's mother that we have not pushed the issue. Our recommendation to her, aside from our advice to let him stay back, has been to remove all pressure and let him perform at his own rate. She just can't see this. On the contrary she seems obsessed with trying to make him into an A student at his present grade level. Nothing else will suffice.

A kindergarten teacher reports:

For several years now our district has been attempting to convince parents of the wisdom of voluntarily postponing putting their young fives into our kindergarten, since Pennsylvania law permits them to come in at such an early age. We kindergarten teachers feel this is a matter of the utmost importance, *having far-reaching effects over all the years of a child's education.* And we are forever grateful for your study which has given us expert scientific facts to back up our belief that children should not start school too young.

A first-grade teacher tells us:

As a first-grade teacher I could cite child after child who has entered first grade but who has not been ready. And I could tell of conference after conference in which I have explained the need for school readiness to parents. "Fall babies" is a term commonly used among first-grade teachers to describe the children whose birthdays fall late in the year.

To help our first-grade parents understand the need for readiness we have had meetings at the beginning of the school year to describe our program and to explain the mental, emotional and social maturities that are necessary for success in first grade. Preschool testing such as advocated by you people would greatly lessen the number of our so-called first-grade failures and would eliminate the heartache felt by both the parents and teachers of children who enter school too young.

Our students are being forced to become little adults, without the opportunity for normal physical, social and emotional growth, without the time to be children. Perhaps these pressures may be the main reasons for the growing number of mentally disturbed children as well as the large number of school drop-outs and delinquents.

A man teacher from Long Island has this to say:

I teach sixth grade. As the financial pressures on families increase, it seems that more mothers wish to work and therefore want to put their children into school at the earliest possible moment. So they start many of them in before they are ready.

By the age of eleven or twelve, some children, especially boys, cannot function at all because they have never, from the beginning, been in a grade which suits their abilities but, rather, have always been placed ahead of the grade where they belong.

I, myself, started kindergarten well before I was five. Things weren't too bad until my sophomore year in high school. I managed till then, but at that point it was almost impossible for me to function.

Please keep hammering out this fact that overplacement can have a deadly effect on a child's whole school performance.

We could multiply these examples endlessly, but this handful will give you the idea that even though you yourself as a parent may have had a bad experience with your school in trying to keep your child back, many many teachers *are* on your side.

And it isn't just the teachers. Child specialists who work with the public schools are also, in many instances, fully aware of the serious problem which unreadiness poses.

A California psychologist, Director of Guidance in the public schools, writes:

For some years now I have been very much concerned about students in our schools who, in my terms, have built "nothing upon nothing" until they have become highly frustrated and defeated inwardly while at the same time school and society's demands continued their exposure to this constant defeat. In so many cases, tracing back early school records, I have been pretty much convinced that the problem was a result of starting formal education prior to being ready.

To try to correct matters, we have all kindergarten teachers bring to our attention within the first few weeks of school any children who appear to be immature and not ready for school in comparison with the rest of the group. Then we go out and observe these youngsters under different situations and later have case conferences concerning them. Where we feel them not actually ready for school, we explain the situation to the parents and leave it up to them to either leave the child in or keep him out another year. Many parents do accept our recommendation and hold their youngsters out the additional year.

The other thing we have done is to meet at each of our schools in the spring at the time of kindergarten registration for the following year, and talk to parents of these entering kindergarteners. We explain a little bit of our kindergarten program, but the primary purpose of the meeting is to more or less explain the "facts of life" concerning readiness for school. We dwell especially on the effects on the younger children who are not ready for school. We make this a pretty personal thing and the results have been quite successful. As a result of these meetings we have probably had in the neighborhood of thirty to forty youngsters each year whom the parents have decided to keep out an additional year.

Or an Iowa psychologist, Director of Special Education, tells us:

For the past eight years I have been testing preschoolers to predict readiness and ability to compete on a successful plane. Recently I completed a survey of these results and found that approximately 70 percent of the children who as preschoolers indicated the possibility of developing difficulties are at present having a hard time in school. Of 628 children whom I've tested, 131 seemed to me as either unready or showing the possibility of other types of problems. Ninety-one (or 69 percent of these potentially problem children) have developed serious school problems.

It has been my belief for some time that educators and psychologists should spend more time in the *preventive* field of school problems of children rather than working long and hard on attempting to correct these difficulties after the pattern has been set.

So for any of you parents who yourselves may already have appreciated the importance of having your child placed in school where he belongs and the importance of having him go more slowly if that seems indicated, we can assure you that you are not alone in your realization. The difficulty lies in the fact that a perceptive teacher, a perceptive parent, a perceptive school principal or child specialist *alone* cannot make the necessary decision. It takes the cooperation of all involved before a really wise and effective decision about any child's schooling can be reached.

## PART TWO

# Behavior Changes with Age

# Chapter 6

## AGES FOUR TO EIGHT AND

## WHAT TO EXPECT

THERE are at least three special things which each parent needs to know if he is going to fully understand his boy or girl. These three main variables are the child's chronological age, his physiological age and his behavior age. (Any parent should, ideally, also know a great deal about his child's basic, inborn individuality or personality, but that is a different story and another book.)

Ideally, perhaps, the three factors of chronological, physiological and behavior age should all go along together. That is, a six-year-old child should have the body of a six-year-old and the behavior of a six-year-old.

It is because not all six-year-olds have reached the six-year-old behavior stage that not all of them behave like six-year-olds and thus are not ready for first grade at the birthday age of six. And that is why it is desirable that each child should have the benefit of a careful behavior examination to see just where he *is* behaving.

However, even without such an examination, there's a lot that a parent can do to draw her own conclusion as to whether or not a child is up to what we expect of a child of his or her chronological age. If you know what kind of behavior is customarily expected of any given age, it helps you to be aware of the fact (when and if it should occur) that your own child is not developing at the expected rate.

Our basic belief that child behavior does develop in a patterned, predictable way, plus careful observation of many children over many years* has motivated us to determine and describe, for the use of parent, teacher and others who work directly with young children, behaviors which we consider most highly characteristic of the various age levels.

If your child is behaving in a way which seems to fit our description of a *younger* age, then you will have reason to suspect that he is immature and may need to proceed in school at a pace somewhat slower than that which the law allows.

We give you here brief descriptions of the ages four to eight. It is important for any of you with children of these (or any) ages not only to be familiar with specific age characteristics of behavior but to appreciate the fact that behavior does change with age in a highly predictable and patterned way. Thus ages when behavior is characterized by good equilibrium—ages when the child tends to get along smoothly within himself and with others—tend to alternate with ages when behavior is jangled and out of equilibrium. Ages when behavior is characteristically expansive and outgoing tend to alternate with ages when it is less expansive and more pulled in.

The following thumbnail sketches will give readers a notion of some of the ways of behaving which characterize the succeeding age levels four through eight years of age.

## The Four-Year-Old

The key word with which we describe the four-year-old girl or boy is "out of bounds." The child of this age is, characteristically, rather wild and exuberant in the way he behaves.

Whatever the situation, he tends to go to what adults consider

* These observations were begun, under the direction of Dr. Arnold Gesell, in the 1930's. For further detail, readers are referred to our earlier books: *Infant and Child in the Culture of Today* (1943), *The Child from Five to Ten* by Gesell and Ilg (1946) and *Child Behavior* by Ilg and Ames (Harper 1955).

extremes. If he laughs, he laughs very loudly. If he shouts, he shouts loudly. If, as he often will, he tells a tall tale, it is a very tall tale indeed. In fact in much of his conversation he seems only slightly influenced by what adults consider to be the truth.

Four, much of the time, tends to be good-natured and friendly, but in a school situation he does not yet show the desire to please which is so characteristic of the good little five-year-old, who dearly wants to do what the adult wants him to. And so the teacher of any four-year-old must still consider the child's abilities, moods, wishes much more than she will when he is five and wants to please *her*.

Four tends to be out of bounds in almost every dimension. Motorwise, like a younger child, he still is extremely active. Not for him long periods of sedentary occupation. He likes to be on the go, and his activity tends to be, at times, rather violent. He is not at all times a respecter of other persons.

Though he can at times, as in nursery school, take his part in group activity, he tends to want to talk when he wants to talk, and his talk is often not only loud but keyed to his own feelings at the moment. He may tell tall tales, exaggerate, express himself profanely—anything for attention. He likes to call attention to himself and to be the center of attention, even unfavorable attention.

All of this out-of-bounds activity has its charming side, and a child of this age can be very amusing if you don't take his behavior too seriously or too moralistically. And though he can be a very good member of a nursery school group, any child (regardless of his age in years) who is behaving like a four-year-old is clearly in no way suited for the even slightly formalized activities of the usual five-year-old kindergarten class.

## The Four-and-a-Half-Year-Old

The four-year-old may be a little bit wild much of the time, but at least he tends to be consistent. You have a pretty good idea, with him, of what to expect. Not so with the typical four-and-a-half-year-old. The most predictable thing about the child of this age tends to be his unpredictability.

The four-and-a-half-year-old boy or girl is beginning to pull in, in his behavior, toward the time when he will be a quiet, capable, matter of fact, consistently "good" five-year-old. But he hasn't reached this time yet and so he varies between being wild and calm, happy and tearful, cooperative and uncooperative.

And just as the adult may not know, from one minute to the next, quite what to expect of him, he himself seems not to know quite what to expect of the world. This is an age when the child has a hard time distinguishing what is true from what is not; what is real from what is make believe.

All of this seems to give him quite a lot of trouble, with himself and with others. Life now has its definite ups and downs. He will worry about something one minute, forget it the next.

The four-and-a-half-year-old can adapt a little better than the four-year-old to the demands of others, can even on occasion do something he doesn't want to just to please. And he can stick to a given task a little better than he did six months earlier. But this is still no age for the average child to be faced with the day in, day out demands of the usual kindergarten routine. He tends to wilt and to go to pieces, to fuss that he doesn't like school and doesn't want to go. And unless the kindergarten curriculum is modified to closely resemble that of a high-powered four-year-old nursery school, it is often not the happiest possible experience for even a quite bright four-and-a-half-year-old.

## THE FIVE-YEAR-OLD

The five-year-old boy or girl has been described correctly as the perfect little kindergartener, and so he turns out to be. Chances are if you have a five-year-old, or an older child who is behaving like five, that kindergarten will be a happy experience for him.

Actually, almost any reasonably favorable situation can turn out to be a happy situation for the five-year-old, for at this age, if ever, the child seems by nature set to find life agreeable. He positively projects good will as he wakes in the morning and proclaims, "Today is going to be my lucky day!" Or, even more constructively, "Today I'm going to do all of the good things and none of the bad things."

Five has correctly been described as secure, stable, capable, reliable. True, it doesn't always work out quite that well, but in general, at home or school, Five prospers by his very determination to please the grown-up. It has been truly said that his mother is the center of the five-year-old's world and his teacher falls not far behind. He WANTS to do what she wants him to. He likes to HELP. He likes to hang around near the adult.

There is something very touching in the trusting way the typical five-year-old will take your hand. In the way he will beam as he tells you interesting things about his life. In the docile way he takes his place and part in the school routine.

Five is not the most adventurous age in the world, and most children of this age like to remain close to home. Most, however, find not too much difficulty in expanding that close world which they enjoy, to include the requirements of kindergarten, with its usually fairly easy demands. The brightest Five in the world is not, as a rule, ready for the wider expanding of horizons and the all-day attendance required by first grade, but most love kindergarten.

In fact, the very goodness and acceptance of things as they are, as opposed to the drive and desire to change things to what you want of them, is one of the clearest behavior characteristics which distinguishes quiet, good, accepting Five from adventurous, daring and not always docile Six. If any of you have a six-year-old who seems to you so much nicer, quieter and better behaved than other Sixes in the neighborhood, do not take it entirely as a credit to your own superior methods of discipline. Rather, at least consider the possibility that your six-year-old may be just a trifle immature.

## FIVE-AND-A-HALF TO SIX YEARS OF AGE

One of the most interesting, clear-cut and easily recognizable—as well as in its own way amusing—age-related changes in behavior is the one which occurs so conspicuously around five-and-a-half years of age.

Along about this time, many perfectly normal little boys and girls undergo such a metamorphosis, such a change for what we normally think of as the "worse," that many and many a mother has remarked, "Oh, how I wish I had my good little five-year-old back again." (Actually she probably doesn't. Most parents have the stamina to face even the bad aspects of growing, maturing, expanding behavior. Few genuinely yearn for the goodness of an earlier, less demanding age.)

What customarily occurs around five-and-a-half years of age, in the normal course of development, is that the child begins to burst out of his self-contained, satisfied, comfortable five-year-old cocoon. His interests, energy and enthusiasm expand till there sometimes seems almost nothing he will not undertake.

He likes to try new things and he likes to come up hard against the world. A five-year-old for whom a play situation goes badly is likely to withdraw and seek the comfort of home and mother. A five-and-a-half to six-year-old may stay and fight things out.

The child of this age tends to be enthusiastic, energetic, eager for new activity and adventure. When things go right, his eyes really shine with enthusiasm at the new experience. When they go wrong, he can be stubborn, contrary, violently hateful.

Like his younger two-and-a-half-year-old self, the five-and-a-half to six-year-old seems to live in an emotional climate of opposite extremes. He loves at one minute, hates at the next. And when things go wrong, as they so often do, he tends to blame his mother. Mother, the person he is most anxious to please when he is five, now is the person he is most likely to blame. Whatever happens that he doesn't like, it's all her fault.

For the typical five-year-old, mother was the center of the

world. Not so at the age which just follows. The five-and-a-half to six-year-old is the center of his own universe and he wants to come first, to be loved most, to get all the attention, to win all the games. It is very hard for a child of this age to lose in any competition— so hard that he is very likely to cheat if cheating is necessary in order to win. He is a poor sport of the first order.

Fortunately, as at so many ages, the most extreme aspects of the typical age behavior are expressed in the safeness of home. Late kindergarten and early first-grade teachers sometimes say that the children in their class behave hardly at all in this way we have just described, or as their mothers say they behave. Probably just as well—since few teachers have the patience to cope with the kind of behavior with which mothers of five-and-a-half to six-year-olds are all too familiar.

The five-and-a-half to six-year-old is often described as being at his very tangled, stubborn, oppositional worst with his mother, and perhaps it's lucky so, since most mothers, discouraged as they may become at times, do have the stamina to cope with this kind of behavior and to look forward hopefully to the possibility of easier years ahead.

School, fortunately, tends to bring out the positive side of six— the expansive, enthusiastic, ready-for-anything vigor which makes the boy or girl of this age—at his best—so delightful a person.

At any rate, any mother who finds that her child as he turns five-and-a-half to six expresses none of the characteristics we have just described but, rather, remains quiet, close to home, amenable, conforming, correct—may do one of two things. She may congratulate herself on her better than average discipline which she may think has kept her child "good" in an often difficult age. Or she may suspect that he is behaving in a way slightly immature for his age and may question his readiness for a first grade which is made up chiefly of boisterous, enthusiastic, expansive and ready-for-anything six-year-olds.

### THE SEVEN-YEAR-OLD

The six-year-old boy or girl quite characteristically seems to expand, sometimes a little too far and to come up too hard against the world around him. Ready for anything, he often takes on more than he can accomplish, and he all too often meets this failure with temper and tears. Only to bounce up, on the following day, with renewed zest and zip.

The typical seven-year-old, on the other hand, sometimes seems almost too pulled in, too undaring, too withdrawn, too quiet and reserved. In his degree of reserve, his lack of expansive drive toward the new, dangerous, different, he reminds us a little of the quiet, close-to-home five-year-old but in few other ways. Five was secure, competent, stable, calm, well-adjusted and, in his somewhat unadventurous way, rather happy about life.

As the boy or girl approaches seven and starts withdrawing, though withdrawal may sound the same self-protective note it did at five, there is much less an air of complacent calm and self-sufficiency. Five sometimes seems not to spread out into the world because he like things where he is. Seven gives the impression of withdrawing because the world is, in some respects, so dreadful and dangerous and unfriendly.

The typical seven-year-old fatigues easily. But it seems to be more than fatigue which gives him such a negative feeling about people and things around him. The child of this age quite typically complains that his teacher doesn't like him and is mean to him; that other kids don't like him and are picking on him. Home is not exempt from his complaints—he tends to think that things in the family are not fair. Other children in the family, he is certain, are treated better than he is and he complains that he NEVER gets his turn.

In fact, some Sevens go so far as to believe that this isn't even their real family, but that they are adopted. All in all, the seven-year-old's list of grievances tends to be long and comprehensive, and he cries at the drop of a hat.

(All, of course, is not negative about the boy or girl of this age. Seven at his best can be thoughtful, determined, persistent, a very nice person to have around the house and very touching in his almost adult seriousness. Good traits as well as bad are all part of the picture of a child operating on a restrained, contemplative, more serious beam than that observed just a few months earlier.)

At any rate, if, in addition to the usual difficulties which age itself brings to the seven-year-old, he has the misfortune to be overplaced in school and thus finds its demands genuinely more than he can meet, life can be bitter indeed. There can be few sadder sights than an immature little seven-year-old, all or most of his baby teeth intact, drooping through a too long and overtiring school day and struggling ineffectually to complete work which he should not have been required to try in the first place.

## THE EIGHT-YEAR-OLD

Seven withdraws, but Eight goes out to meet the world. In fact we often think of the eight-year-old as being expansive, speedy and evaluative. This can, of course, lead to trouble on occasion since the child of this age sometimes uses less than good judgment in his expanding, and tries to do more than he actually can perform. He covers much ground and covers it speedily but not always well. Then in comes his evaluative ability to make trouble for him—he reviews what he has done and is often less than satisfied.

Then he asks, obliquely, for assurance. "It's not very good, is it?" Or, eight years old though he may be, he just breaks down and cries in disappointment over his own unsatisfactory performance.

The typical Eight is especially vulnerable where his mother is concerned. He is highly sensitive to her moods and feelings, and wants very much that things be good between them. She, however, is the person expected to do most of the adapting, and many mothers do find the extreme emotional demands of the eight-year-old exhausting. "He haunts me," they complain.

However, happily, except for occasional bursts of crying and a great sensitivity wherever his mother is concerned, the eight-year-old tends to view his world with a good deal of positive enthusiasm.

Perhaps we can see Eight most clearly if we contrast him with his seven-year-old self. This is perhaps one of the greatest contrasts provided all along the way. When your quiet, thoughtful, pensive, retiring and, admittedly often complaining, seven-year-old suddenly bursts out into a new world of exploring, enthusiastic, adventurous action, there need be little question, even without consulting the calendar, that he has turned eight.

Clear as these age changes tend to be (both in our own minds and in actual living practice) it is essential for anyone dealing with young children to realize that what we have described is merely what tends to happen *on the average*. These are the ways that behavior changes from age to age, and on the average this is the timetable which children follow.

But—and this is what we have tried to stress all along—each child has his own individual timetable. Some are ahead of, some are behind, the group average. It is when your five-year-old behaves more like a four, when your six-year-old behaves more like a five, that he shows himself unready for five-year-old kindergarten or six-year-old first-grade work.

# Chapter 7

## EYES AND TEETH TELL

## THEIR STORY TOO

AS we have pointed out in the preceding chapter, a child's behavior age tends to correspond with both his birthday age and his body's age. Since this is the case, even when a behavior examination or careful estimate of any given child's behavior age is not available, IF we know his birthday or calendar age, and if we know his physiological age, we may assume that very likely his behavior age is at that same level.

Child specialists usually agree that one of the best measures of physiological age is an X ray of the wrist bones. This measure is in most cases not available. But there is one clue which *is* available to anybody who wants to look and that is the child's level of teething, a further good index to his physiological age.

It is not that we are primarily concerned with physiological age as such. A child's teething, which is one clue to his body's age, *could* be below the average for a child of his years without necessarily interfering with his school performance, *if it were not for the fact* that slow teething tends to go along with slow development of behavior.

Teething has been a matter of interest, sometimes of pain and sometimes of pride, to most mothers ever since a child's baby days. As the time for school beginning comes along, the child's teething can be one of a parent's best clues as to how rapidly he is developing.

We know when, on the average, it is reasonable to expect the first of a child's second teeth, and which ones they probably will be. Usually the first teeth a child loses are his lower central incisors (the two lower middle front teeth). The new ones usually come in when he is around five-and-a-half to six years of age. At six come the six-year-molars. Next, the child ordinarily loses his upper central incisors, and the new ones come in when he is around six-and-a-half years old. Around six-and-a-half, too, most children get their lower lateral incisors (the teeth on each side of the two middle ones). At seven, the upper lateral incisors erupt.

Now what does all of this mean? There are, admittedly, many exceptions. A child's *behavior* can be ahead of or behind his teething. But as a rule, if your child's teething is right where we would expect for his age, it's fairly safe to say that his behavior is probably also coming along at the usual or average rate.

If teething is markedly ahead of the average, behavior, too, may be somewhat advanced. This in most cases will be all to the good. As our schools are set up today, the child with a plus edge on maturity tends to prosper.

The thing for parents to watch, and perhaps to be warned about, is teething which is *behind* the usual or expected time schedule. Thus, if your five-and-a-half or six-year-old has not lost his two lower middle teeth and thus, of course, doesn't have his new ones, or if your six-and-a-half-year-old doesn't have his second upper middle teeth, chances are that behavior as well as teething may be behind the average.

And what this means is that the child may not be ready for the work of the grade for which his birthday age supposedly readies him. Even more of a warning signal is the first or second-grader who still has all of his baby teeth firmly rooted with no sign of loosening. Such a level of teething is indeeed a sign that such a child needs to go slowly in school.

Readers may be interested to know to what extent we have found the speed or slowness of a child's teething to fit in with his success or failure in school. In a group of eighty Weston, Connecticut, kindergarten children, who had been entered in school on the basis of age rather than on the basis of behavior maturity, we found the following correlations:

OF THOSE AHEAD OF SCHEDULE IN TEETHING:
    60 percent were in the top group academically
    36 percent were doing well or fairly well
    4 percent were doing badly
OF THOSE BEHIND SCHEDULE IN TEETHING:
    6 percent only were in the top group in school
    40 percent were questionable
    54 percent did repeat or in our estimation should have repeated

These findings are, in our experience, fairly typical. That is, there appears to be a close correlation between physiological maturity (as evidenced by the level of teething) and behavior maturity. The child with advanced teething *tends* to be advanced, also, in his behavior.

So far as teeth go, it is the actual physical structure of the teeth which we have described, and this is something that the parent can observe.

Eyes, too have their tale to tell, but this is a much more technical story, concerned more with their function and behavior than with their structure. And this is not something which we would expect parents to evaluate in any detail.

However, we'd like to have you know that this behavior *can* and *should* be evaluated. In fact, the main thing we'd like to tell readers about eyes is that just as you send your child, regularly, to the dentist *whether he is having trouble with his teeth or not,* so you should also send him to the visual specialist for regular checkups. We would like to have every child visit the eye specialist routinely as a matter of course, just as he visits his dentist. Good vision care should not be the responsibility of the school any more than is good dental care.

Ideally, each child should have a careful visual examination given by a skilled private practitioner before he starts school, and each year thereafter. Visual specialists all over the country are becoming increasingly aware that there is much they can do to help children in school use their eyes more effectively. They are also coming to realize that eyes do not exist in a vacuum—they are part of the growing child. We hope eventually to develop methods of perceptual training that can be used in the schools. We also hope to see school curriculums improved so that they do not make as excessive a demand of children's eyes as many do now.

Not only do we find that a shocking percentage of children have some sort of vision difficulties, but even worse is the fact that many experience difficulties who do not need to under ideal conditions. Some children who have potentially good vision need some help (as temporary or developmental lenses, or visual training) along the way in order to develop effectively. Others are pushed into visual difficulty by being given near work too soon—as in the case of children who are pushed into early (preschool) reading before they show by their own demand and interest that they are ready. Still others may have started to go off the track visually, but their visual behavior could be improved or corrected by temporary lens help or visual training.

Even some children who appear to be getting on well at home or at school could be helped by better learning conditions set up in school to use their eyes more effectively and more comfortably than they now are doing.

If you cannot get the kind of visual help for your child which we suggest, don't be too discouraged. This whole area of understanding and doing something about child vision is a new one. Great strides and advances in our knowledge have been made in the last dozen years or so, but we are still just at the beginning.

A forthcoming book from our Institute will tell you in detail some of the things we now know about children's vision which you as parents should know. One of the things which this book sets forth is that the child's visual behavior, like any other aspect of his behavior, does develop in a patterned way through a series of definite predictable stages which can be understood by the specialist. Thus we know, for instance, that Five is a focal age visually. Ocular fixation is superior to ocular pursuit. Many five-year-olds are not ready to use their eyes in the way that is necessary for reading.

The five-and-a-half-year-old is more experimental visually than he was six months earlier. His big problem, so far as reading goes, is that he easily loses his visual orientation and thus may often *reverse* his letters. By six, however, eyes are more ready for reading. Monocular behavior is giving way to a new binocularity and the child is much better at following, though he still is likely to lose his place.

Seven's big problem, as far as school is concerned, is that though he can see things on the board, or can work at his desk, he finds it difficult to make the visual adaptations required in copying from the board, though many second-grade teachers require this activity.

Each age has its new visual abilities and its new problems. The more we understand these, the better job we can do of fitting our requirements to what the child is able to do. We have told you about them, briefly, so that you will realize that you cannot teach a child anything you may wish to at any time you want to. His body and his behavior must, for any given behavior, have developed to a certain stage of maturity before that behavior is possible, or at least safe and comfortable. No matter how hard you push and no matter how hard the child tries, successful behavior must wait for maturity. It's not all up to you.

And for reading behavior especially, that performance so essential to effective school work, eyes must be ready before we can expect success.

Eyes you can in many instances do something about. Teeth you won't as a rule do too much about (except naturally to see that your child practices good dental hygiene). Their special interest for you, in this context, is that they can be a clue to you as to how rapidly, or slowly, your child's body, and by the same token his behavior, is maturing.

# Chapter 8

## BEHAVIOR DOES MAKE SENSE

BY now readers will have gathered that we think that a child's behavior does make sense. We have discovered, in fifty or so years of carefully controlled research, during which time we have examined tens of thousands of children, that the behavior of most children is not only patterned but highly predictable. Even from the way a child behaves in infancy, we can, as a rule, tell a good deal about what his behavior will be later in life. Certainly by the time he has reached kindergarten age it is quite possible for a skilled observer to make pretty safe predictions as to what a certain child's behavior will be in the years to come.

We must admit, however, that not everybody agrees with this point of view. Happily a great many people, including most parents and many teachers, believe as we do that much of any child's behavior is determined genetically. He is the kind of child he is because, to a large extent, he was born that way. How you treat a child can have a strong influence on the way he turns out—and will very likely determine whether or not he is able to express his best and finest potentials. But in the long run it is the child's inherited potentials rather than the way you treat him which make him the kind of person he is. Your task is to help him become most fully himself.

Parents of large families find it especially natural to hold this point of view. No matter how hard they try to make all of their children conform to some beautiful ideal, they still find that each one turns out to be remarkably unique and different from every other one.

As one mother of seven recently wrote to us:

Since I became the mother of seven children I have discarded many of my earlier notions. I used to think that children were just lumps of clay which could be molded to suit their parents' wishes. Now I know better.

Our first girl, Betty, even now at seventeen years of age is *still* stubborn, difficult, hard to get on with as she was when a baby. Our first boy, Neddie, was just the opposite. He ate well, slept well, got on well with everybody, right from the beginning. And the same can be said of his younger sister, Amy. She was a happy and very active little baby. And now she is twelve and still very active and happy. I still enjoy her even at this (ugh!) pre-teen junior high stage.

And so on through the family. Our last baby, a girl, has been a joy to everybody right from the beginning. So there you have it: a first girl, stubborn, hard to handle, hard to live with from the word go. The second is quiet and not much bothered by what is fashionable. The third is energy in a tidy package, full of sympathy and love. The fourth is slow moving and slow to try new things but does like to be in fashion. The fifth is determined, kind, fun and talks a blue streak. Six is a bit spoiled but knows what he wants to do and how it should be done. Seven is a complete joy.

With each child we did what seemed to work, and what worked with one by no means worked with the next. It is a hard lesson to learn that you have to take what you get in children, that it is not all up to you how they turn out and that the environment cannot greatly change the inborn characteristics of any child.

It is our finding that behavior is to a large extent a function of structure (that is, that people behave as they do because of the way their bodies and brains are constructed). This means that you cannot appreciably hurry or speed up the time at which your child walks, or talks, or is ready to read and write and adjust to the demands of a school situation.

If you believe as we do that the best environment, the best food, the finest teaching, the most loving care will not make a child do any of these things *until* his organism is fully ready, you will find it easy to wait until he *is* ready for the school situation.

On the other hand, if you believe that it all, or much of it, depends on you, you will be anxious to teach academic subjects in the preschool years, and you will be eager to start your child in school at the youngest possible age because you will believe that the sooner you start, the sooner he will learn, regardless of his state of readiness.

Which point of view you hold will also determine the extent to which you believe early behavior is predictive and prophetic of later behavior. Those who agree with our point of view (which is called the developmental point of view) believe with us that a behavior test given at a young age can predict to a pretty good extent what later behavior will be like.

Probably the majority of investigators, even when they do not consider infant tests to be highly predictive, do believe that as the child grows older, tests become more predictive and therefore do agree that preschool tests have some predictive value. And most agree that tests given as the child approaches school age can be highly predictive.

It may seem to some of you not to make too much difference what your philosophy of child behavior is so long as you do a good job bringing up your children. This may be right, in a way, but sober second thought will probably make you realize that what you *believe* about child behavior will strongly influence what you *do* about it.

If you believe that the environment can do almost anything, you will want to get to work hard and early to try to make your child into a perfect specimen of some type predetermined by your own wishes. If, with us, you believe that you can mold and inflect behavior but that you cannot determine either the shape it takes or the rate at which it will grow, you will be more relaxed. And you will blame yourself less if things turn out less than perfectly.

"Your practical advice is great," a young mother told us recently. "It's just your theories I'm against." This mother was wrong in thinking that the two can be separated. Almost every bit of practical advice which we give parents stems directly from our theoretical position.

This is particularly true with respect to the child's school behavior. Our theoretical position leads us to make every possible effort not to start a child in school till his total behavior picture indicates that he is fully ready. It leads us to let him, within reason, follow his own pace in school—if he needs to repeat, we let him. It helps us to recognize that not every child is suited to that top division. It warns us not to work too hard, in the preschool years, to teach a child things he will pick up quite naturally when he is a few years older.

It leads us also to recognize that not every child will be academically gifted. Some children are inevitably better at living than they are at learning. Some children who are close to normal intelligence still need to be taught in a very special way and may not fit into the regular classroom. And, when the time comes, not every child will turn out to be college material.

Just as you try to recognize your own child's unique personality in other ways, also try to understand him as a school child. Help him to do his best, but keep in mind that not every child is by nature a ready or rapid scholar.

This point of view, that behavior is largely determined by inherent forces (even though of course it can be strongly influenced by the environment), that it develops in a patterned way and that later behavior can to a large extent be predicted from early behavior, lies at the basis of our method of testing for school readiness.

Thus it is our contention that graded behavior tests, given at the time when a child is approaching or has presumably reached school age, can tell us not only whether he is at the time ready to start school, but can predict, within fairly close limits, how well he will do later on. That is, the child who gives evidence of being ready for kindergarten will in all likelihood continue to be ready, if he proceeds evenly a year at a time, for the grades which follow.

Thus behavior, in at least many cases, does proceed in a patterned, predictable way and individuality is, to a large extent, understandable and predictable too. Any parent who is able to look at his child as an individual, and above all to look at his child's body as the source of much of his behavior (rather than believing as some do that we can make any child into almost anything if only we try hard enough and use the correct treatment) is able to give his child a tremendous advantage with regard to his life in school as elsewhere.

It is our hope that eventually all parents will know enough about constitution and physical type to recognize the kind of child they have produced and to treat him accordingly. This knowledge will be handed on to the child himself, as he grows older, so that he can better understand himself.

As readers familiar with our earlier books will know, we follow the system of constitutional psychology set forth by William Sheldon.* According to this system, behavior is a function of structure and the human individual behaves as he does largely because of the way he is structured. Remaining reasonably consistent throughout the life span, the actual physical structure of the body can be a clue as to what kind of behavior one can and cannot expect of each person.

Though there do not actually exist different distinct "types" of body build, we can identify three chief physical components. These three components are—endomorphy, mesomorphy, ectomorphy. Each person actually represents a unique combination of these three different components, but in most people one or the other component tends to predominate. Thus we often loosely speak as if there were only three types of individual.

The person in whom endomorphy predominates is referred to as an *endomorph*. These individuals have large stomachs and livers, that is, large digestive viscera, and are usually fat. They are soft and spherical in shape. Their behavior is characterized by extreme relaxation and love of comfort. They are sociable, love food, love people and are gluttons for affection. In school such children are usually good-natured, friendly and sociable, but are not particu-

* William H. Sheldon, *Varieties of Temperament* (Harper, 1942).

larly competitive and don't particularly care about being outstanding. They often do not try as hard, or get as good marks, as their parents and teachers think they could and should.

The *mesomorph,* in contrast, has big bones, a well-developed heart and circulatory system, and heavy muscles. He is hard, firm, upright and relatively strong. Blood vessels are large and the skin is relatively thick, with large pores. In his behavior, muscular activity and vigorous bodily assertion predominate. He loves exercise and activity, loves to dominate. In school he usually gets along well with other children but as a leader, rather than a follower. He tends to be highly competitive. Discipline may be a problem since, especially in the earlier grades, he finds it hard to sit still for long periods of time. His posture is good and he tends to be good at and much interested in athletics and competitive sports.

The *ectomorph,* in extreme contrast, is the thin, fragile, linear person, flat of chest and with long, slender, poorly muscled or "pipestem" arms and legs. His behavior shows restraint, inhibition, oversensitiveness and a desire for concealment. He shrinks from even ordinary school occasions. Since the ectomorphic child tends to be immature for his age as compared to other children, and if bright is often much interested in and good at academic activities, he is apt to be—unless careful attention is paid to real readiness —the child who is entered in school too young. He is from then on likely to be the youngest but the brightest in the class, always overplaced by our standards and never really fitting in or getting the most out of school. But if this is pointed out, somebody always counters with the fact of his good marks. He "can" do the work, even though he doesn't fit or enjoy school or get the most out of it.

The ectomorph has the further problem, in addition to often being younger than the others, of not being very sociable and also not very athletic. He is the very child whom we would like to see taking a slightly more deliberate course in school so that he would not always be the smallest, youngest, smartest person in his class.

Each of these three types of individual, because of his own

special physical structure, has different drives, different responses, different interests, from each of the others. Sheldon sums up these differences by saying that the endomorph exercises and attends in order to eat; the mesomorph eats and attends in order to exercise and the ectomorph eats and exercises in order to attend. He adds that it is probable that we will never be able to understand all of our children until we have first learned to tell them apart.

*PART THREE*

# How to Determine Readiness

# Chapter 9

## DEVELOPMENTAL PLACEMENT

## TESTS

SINCE the theme of this book is that children should not, ideally, begin school until they are fully *ready* to do so, we'd like to give you specific information as to how you know when a child *is* ready.

There are two outstanding ways for determining readiness. One is the simple direct kind of evaluation which the knowing parent, teacher or child specialist makes with regard to a child's level of performance.

It doesn't really take a specialist to spot immaturity in most cases. Mothers so often comment, "Timmy just isn't as mature as the other five-year-olds in the neighborhood," or "Betty is so baby-ish compared to what her sisters were at her age."

Teachers say the same thing over and over again: "I have half a dozen children in my room who don't belong here. They just are not as mature as the rest."

Many people have the experience, or the instinct or intuition to recognize immaturity when they meet it. Others—mothers of small families, teachers just beginning—may need outside clues.

This is the main thing we would recommend to parents: Check, either on your own knowledge of the way children of different ages behave, *or* check our descriptions of the ages to see whether or not your school beginner is behaving in a general way at or above his age, or below that age. If it seems to you that a child's behavior is below that which would be expected of a child his age, then it is very important (if behavior tests which would decide the question are lacking) to try to be *sure* in your own mind that he is ready for the work of the grade to which age assigns him.

The child specialist, on the other hand, has two ways of determining whether or not a child is ready for school. He, too, like the experienced parent or teacher has a very good sense of whether or not any given boy or girl shows or does not show the maturity we would expect at his chronological age.

But since such a judgment must remain subjective at best, the child specialist has a second way of judging readiness. In our case, this way consists of giving the Gesell Developmental Screening Test to each child who is by age ready to start kindergarten (if the school system provides a kindergarten), the full Developmental Placement Test before he begins first grade if there is no kindergarten.

Since it is by no means our aim to ask parents to try to test their own children, we shall not describe these tests in any great or technical detail. However, though it is not usually wise for parents to try to test their own children, readers may be interested to know something about the Gesell School Readiness (or as we prefer to call them Developmental Placement) Tests.* We hope eventually that these tests, or others like them, may be given to all school children at the time of their entrance to school, and at any time thereafter when there is any question as to what grade or group they belong in.

It is important to keep in mind that school readiness tests are not the same thing as intelligence tests. Intelligence can easily be measured by any of the good intelligence tests now available. We

---

* Any parent who would like to know more about our tests is referred to *School Readiness* by Frances L. Ilg and Louise Bates Ames (Harper & Row, 1965).

use most often the WISC (Wechsler Intelligence Scale for Children).*

Our behavior or developmental tests measure not intelligence per se but rather behavior maturity. As we've noted earlier, a child can be bright and mature, bright and immature, less bright but mature, less bright and immature. Any of these combinations is possible.

That is, our tests tell whether a child's general behavior is at, below or above his chronological age. Our stand is that it is the child's behavior age (not his age in years or his I.Q.) that is the best guide to time of school entrance and subsequent promotion.

From our examinations, over the years, of many thousands of children, we know pretty well what the normal or expected behavior of a child of any given age will be. Tests which we use to make such a determination include primarily eye-hand coordination and verbal tests. These tests tell us the age level at which a child responds to simple set tasks.

These tasks or test situations include the following: writing name, date, address and numbers; the copy of such simple forms as a circle, cross, square, triangle, divided rectangle and diamond; the completing of what we call an Incomplete Man figure; tests which give evidence of how clear the child's conception of right and left may be; tests called Monroe Visual One and Visual Three which indicate how well a child can match or recall special forms; seeing how many animals he can name in a minute's time and asking the child to tell what he prefers to do at home and at school.

As we say, it is not necessary and probably not desirable for parents to know how to administer such tests. But to give you an idea of what kinds of things we expect at different ages, we shall discuss briefly the printing of name, address and numbers, and the response to two of the most significant of the tests—copy circle and completing the Incomplete Man.

* David Wechsler, *Wechsler Intelligence Scale for Children* (New York: The Psychological Corporation, 1949).

The extent to which their child prints name (or letters) and numbers is something which many parents like to observe. Many children are able to print their first name at five years of age or before, and we expect the child who is developing at an average rate to be able to print his, or her, first name at or soon after five-and-a-half years of age. We expect the child to be able to print both names by the time he is six. (At six he can print his last name on request but he does this spontaneously at seven.) Cursive writing of both names, however, does not come in till eight years of age, size of printed letters is not consistent until seven.

Address, including street, number, city and state, is not given till eight years of age by girls, nine by boys.

Many, though by no means all, children can write their numbers up to five by the time they are five years old. Five-and-a-half writes numbers to ten. Numbers one to eleven or more (up through nineteen) are not expected till children are fully six. Boys can write numbers up to twenty when they are six but many girls need to be six-and-a-half before they can get up to twenty or above.

Copying a circle may not seem a particularly telling bit of behavior, and yet from the way a child performs this simple task we can rate his response as falling anywhere from eighteen months to six years or older. Thus an eighteen-monther responds to the request to imitate* a circle by scribbling, usually obliquely. The two-year-old can scribble in a rather circular fashion. By three, however, most are past the scribble stage and can imitate a circular stroke and stop after the first time around.

The child's circle at this time, though large and wobbly, is most often begun at the top and drawn in the same direction in which a right-handed adult draws, that is counterclockwise. However, from three-and-a-half years following, when the child copies the circular form, he tends to start at the bottom and go around in a clockwise direction. And it is not till around five years of age for girls, five-

---

* At the earliest ages the child is asked to imitate the circle, cross and other forms which he sees the examiner make. At later ages he is asked to copy them from a pictured form.

and-a-half for boys, that the circle is again drawn from the top down and in a counterclockwise direction. (These and similar changes in behavior occur as a result of growth changes which at present are not fully understood.)

Thus if your five-year-old girl, your five-and-a-half-year-old boy, when asked to copy a circle, still starts at the bottom and/or draws clockwise, he is showing that, for this test situation at least, he is not responding up to his age.

This, or other behavior in which a child is not responding up to his age, is not by any means necessarily a sign of low intelligence, or of anything to worry about. But it is a clue that this child is showing an immaturity at least in this specific test situation.

The same sort of observation can be made for the other forms which we ask a child to copy. And it is not just the way in which he copies the individual form, but also the size of the forms and the way he arranges them on the page and in relation to each other which gives the experienced examiner the clues he needs in determining the age at which the individual child is responding.

A second test which very clearly tells the age level of response is the Incomplete Man Test, pictured in Figure 1. As this shows, the Incomplete Man figure consists of the unfinished figure of a man. This includes one arm and hand, one leg and foot, nose, mouth, hair and ear on one side, and half of the neck and tie—that is, it includes a model for all missing parts except the eyes.

As the child grows older, he adds an increasing number of parts. However it is not so much the number of parts he adds, as it is the way he draws the parts, which indicates his maturity. Again, though we do not advise parents to try testing their own children, readers may be interested to know some of the kinds of change which take place in the response to the Incomplete Man test as the child matures.

As Figure 2 indicates, the following age changes take place:

The added arm, which at first (say around three to three-and-a-half years of age) tends to be placed too low, be pointed downward and be of too long a length, gradually moves up on the body line,

*Figure 1*
*Incomplete Man Test Form*

turns to point upward and becomes shorter till it matches in size, angle and placement the arm already provided.

Eyes which at first are scribbles, later become large and round, then small and round, then oval with pupils and, eventually, eyebrows and occasionally lashes are added. Hair, which at first is too long, and tends to go too far around the head (even at four-and-a-half years under the chin) gradually becomes shorter and covers less space. The ear is gradually better placed and of a more accurate shape.

At the neck area, the very young child (of preschool age) often adds nothing or merely continues the body line. By five years of age, the majority of children add a line for the neck and by six many start to struggle with the tie. By seven, neck and tie may be the first parts added.

Around four to four-and-a-half years of age many children add a bellybutton. For the child five years old or older, a bellybutton is considered a sign of clear immaturity, since by five many children have given up the extreme interest in genitals, bathrooms and bellybuttons which are so strong in many at four.

And so, not only are more parts added but, as the child matures, the added parts increasingly resemble the parts already provided.

For these and all other tests in our battery, norms are available which can tell the trained examiner just the age at which any given child is behaving.* This is what we call his *behavior* age, and it is the behavior age, not the age in years, which tells us what grade in school any child is ready for.

Right here we'd like to answer a question which parents often ask. They ask, often slyly, "Yes, but what if I should read up on your tests and then teach my child how to respond to them, how would you know if he were really mature, or just had been taught how to make a mature response?"

This really doesn't present the problem which some people fore-

* Frances L. Ilg and Louise Bates Ames, *School Readiness* New York (Harper & Row, 1965).

2 YRS. 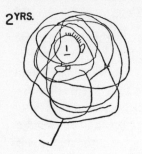  2½ YRS.   3 YRS.

3½ YRS.   4 YRS.   4½ YRS.

5 YRS.   5½ YRS.   6 YRS.

7 YRS.   8 YRS.   9 YRS.

*Figure 2*
*Age Changes in Response to Incomplete Man Test*

see. It is true that with *great* effort, a parent might teach a child who is not quite ready to do so on his own, how to draw a circle from the top down and counterclockwise; might possibly teach him how to add a mature arm or ear, to leave out the bellybutton for the Incomplete Man. Or the most customary bit of teaching is to teach the child who is not quite ready to do so on his own to draw a triangle.

Actually it is most difficult to do this until the child is close to ready to give the mature response on his own. But say that you *could* do it, the total response to any test is so complex, and is made up of so many parts, that it would be almost impossible to cover *all* the points involved.

As we have noted, it is not so much just the child's performance as it is his process—the way he performs—how he holds his pencil, the way he sits at the examining table for instance—which indicates to the experienced examiner the age level of performance. Or, in the Incomplete Man response, it is not just the number of parts added so much as their direction, placement, size and shape which tell the trained examiner what he needs to know.

And, furthermore, the child who has been coached is very likely to give himself away: "Every night I practice how to make a triangle;" "I mustn't put in the bellybutton," he mutters to himself as he performs.

So say that a parent should have the poor judgment and the luck to teach his four-year-old to add a five-year-old *arm* to the Incomplete Man, there is still the matter of the hair, ear, eyes, neck, leg and foot. And any parent with the knowledge to give all the instruction necessary would be almost certain to have respect enough for the tests not to try such a pointless endeavour.

Another example—take the copy forms test. Even should a parent wish to study each of the forms and then wish to struggle to teach his immature child to respond in a manner above his normal untutored potential, there is still the matter of order of drawing, of consistency of size, of placement on the page. Actually it would be an almost unteachable task to *teach* a child to respond above his age on our behavior tests.

And even if you could do it, the child would then give himself away just in the way he holds his pencil, sits at the table, talks and moves as he responds. We can guarantee, it is almost impossible for a parent to beat or to cheat a battery of behavior tests.

Now—who do we see as using developmental placement tests and what use should they make of them?

*Parents* should not be expected to examine their own children. They aren't trained for it and it is not their responsibility. However, even though the average parent is not a physician, he (or she) makes many observations as to his child's state of health. And the same is true for the child's behavior level. The interested parent can note instances of immaturity, when they exist, in his child or children.

*Teachers,* unless they are specifically trained and designated to fill the role of examiner, will in most instances not do a substantial amount of examining. Nevertheless there is much that they *can* do.

Someone has remarked that there is no better instrument for spotting immaturity than a skilled teacher, and we agree. Thus since experienced teachers are quite naturally, in the course of their everyday teaching, making observations as to the maturity or immaturity of their pupils, it seems fair to us to put examining tools into their hands. This does not mean that we expect every teacher to become a psychologist. It does mean that a skilled teacher can, within reason, apply developmental tests, if she so wishes, to her pupils.

Such testing will in many instances merely confirm her own observations but it will have the advantage of objectifying these observations in her own mind. It also gives her objective data which she can show to parents, on the one hand, and to her principal on the other, to support her feelings that some of her pupils may need to be placed in a grade or group other than the one to which age might assign him.

And now for the person who will in most school systems be doing the major amount of testing for readiness. This person will be the *Developmental Examiner,* or in school systems which are fully developmentally oriented, the *Developmental Guidance Co-ordinator.*

The role of Developmental Examiner is a new one in our schools, and just how it will take shape in the years to come nobody knows for sure. Until this role does take on a little more shape and uniformity than it has at present, there may be considerable variation from one school community to another, not only in what this person will do but even in just who he will be.

In some school systems, the school psychologist, if developmentally oriented, may be the person to do developmental testing. In some, it may be a guidance counselor or social worker.

We ourselves have had perhaps the greatest success in those schools where the principal has chosen an effective, experienced, primary school teacher, relieved her from her usual teaching duties and allowed her to receive special training in developmental testing.

The advantage of having a person who has had actual teaching experience is that such an individual can perhaps work most effectively with the classroom teacher in the initial grouping of all children once they have been tested, and in the regrouping of some which is often necessary once school is underway.

As we envisage the work of this Developmental Examiner, or Developmental Guidance Coordinator, in a school where developmental testing and developmental grouping is just starting, her task would go somewhat as follows:

In the spring of the year all incoming kindergarten pupils would be given a very brief examination (consisting chiefly of copy forms and completing the Incomplete Man). Parents of those children who are clearly unready for any kind of kindergarten experience would be advised to have their children wait another year. Other children would be grouped in from two to four groups for kindergarten the coming fall, the young-behaving groups still needing more of a nursery-school experience, the older-behaving groups being ready for more of a usual kindergarten experience.

Also in the spring, all children currently in kindergarten could be examined with the full behavior examination to determine whether they need to repeat kindergarten, be placed in a five-and-a-half-year-old group, or move right on to first grade the coming fall.

And so on, the examiner gradually examining all children in the first five grades as rapidly as time permitted, and adjusting their grade or group placement if the need appears.

Getting any school started would be a somewhat time-consuming matter, but once the whole process had gotten going, the major examining and grouping would be done on the newly-entering students each year, and then the Examiner would gradually have increasing time free to examine children who provided problems in school, and to work where she was needed.

A Developmental Examiner, or Developmental Guidance Co-ordinator would, as we envisage the role, become not only an invaluable liaison officer between parents and school, but could and should become the principal's right-hand man. And could also be the person whom teachers could consult when things went wrong. We envisage such a position as being full-time in each school of around 500-600 pupils (grades kindergarten to fifth). This position is now being tried out in pilot form in our present research.

# Chapter 10

## HOW PARENTS CAN

## RECOGNIZE UNREADINESS

## AND OVERPLACEMENT

THOUGH we have just told you in some detail about our school readiness tests and what they can tell us about any given child's readiness or unreadiness, it is not our hope to make expert diagnosticians of all our readers. The final diagnosis will in most instances be the responsibility of the school personnel or, if the school is lucky enough to have one, of the Developmental Examiner. But there are many clues which can be warning signs to any parent seriously concerned about his or her child's schooling.

Of course IF your child loves school, gets good grades, gets on well with his friends and seems reasonably well adjusted at home, if you and his teacher agree that things are fine and if nobody from the school at any time has hinted that he might do better in a lower grade, you should not borrow trouble and fret about your child's grade placement.

However, there are many perfectly normal children who fall short of this happy ideal. Not because of anything inherently wrong or inadequate about themselves, but simply because somebody has made the mistake of taking the law (or the custom) too literally and assuming that a child who is six in October (or November or December or whatever date your local rule dictates) is inevitably ready for the work of first grade, simply because he has reached a certain calendar age.

Thus, we know that there are many of you who *are* anxious, who *do* wonder. Here are a few questions which you may wish to ask yourself about your child and his response to school. If you find that you answer many of these questions with a "Yes," chances are that your boy or girl may be in a grade above the one in which he truly belongs:

1. Does your child dislike school?

2. Does he complain a great deal that "it's too hard"?

3. Does he have great difficulty in completing the written work assigned in class?

4. Does he seem unduly fatigued when he gets home from school?

5. Has there been any marked change for the worse in his home behavior and in his disposition since he started school?

6. Is he a "different" child in summer when school responsibilities have been removed?

7. Does he have terrible trouble, almost every day, in getting ready for school?

8. Does he complain of stomach-aches, or is he actually sick to his stomach before he goes to school in the morning?

9. Has any marked change for the worse in his health taken place since he started school? Thus, does a normally healthy child suddenly begin to have a series of colds, one after another?

10. Have any of his home routines taken a marked turn for the worse since he started school? For instance, does he eat less well, have trouble in sleeping, exhibit a return to bed-wetting after having been dry at night?

11. Has a normally "good" child suddenly become rebellious, difficult, quarrelsome, cranky at home once school has started?

12. Does your child get much less good school marks than you and the teacher think he is capable of?

13. Does his teacher assure you that he "could do better" if only he would try harder?

14. Does he have trouble socially, either in class or on the playground?

15. Are most or many of his friends chosen from children in a lower grade?

16. Is his teething considerably behind that of other boys and girls in his class?

17. Does he look out of place in the classroom? (This refers not to physical size. Children may quite normally be larger or smaller than the average.) But does he look and act much more babyish than the others?

18. Does a normally "good" child find it terribly difficult to behave in class? Are there constant complaints from the school that he had to be reprimanded, was made to sit out in the hall or had to be sent to the principal's office?

19. Does he do desperate things at school as, for instance, not finishing his paper and then scribbling all over it?

20. Does he find it unduly difficult in class to wait for his turn, speak only when he's supposed to, refrain from "bothering" his classmates?

21. Does he daydream in class, or fail to pay attention, to an extent which the teacher considers unreasonable?

22. Has the teacher or anyone at school suggested to you that your child really is not up to the work of his present grade and that he would be better off in a lower class?

23. Last and perhaps most important of all, does he seem to you babyish for his age compared to other children that same age, or compared to the way his brothers and sisters behaved when they were his age?

Keep in mind that not all children love school at all times. Nor are all normal children completely well adjusted at either home or school all of the time. Far less than perfection can be perfectly normal.

But if you find that you must answer "Yes" to even four or five of the questions listed above, chances are that your boy or girl may be in serious trouble at school and that something needs to be done about it.

Spotting overplacement is not as a rule a tremendously difficult task for the perceptive parent. An overplaced child is a child in trouble, and sensitive parents are usually good at recognizing that.

Deciding whether or not your child is ready to begin school (kindergarten or first grade as the case may be) is somewhat harder. Making such a decision should be the task of the specialist. We look forward to the time when it will be. But in the meantime, your guide will have to be a combination of your own sensitive parental judgment and the advice of the school.

Whether the starting grade in question be kindergarten or first grade, if your child seems to you *babyish for his age*, not up to the other children his same age, this in itself is a clear warning sign.

Chances are you'll have your own good instinct about this. Most parents seem to. If you haven't been thinking in terms of behavior age and all of this is new to you, you might reread chapter six and see if you can spot your own child in the descriptions given there. If your five-year-old seems, on the basis of these descriptions, to be more like a four, if your six-year-old seems more like a five, you already have a warning.

The kindergarten (or first-grade) teacher may help you. Ideally there should be some sort of preregistration situation or experience in the spring before kindergarten starts which will enable the experienced teacher to spot special cases of immaturity.

If the school has no Developmental Examiner, if your own instinct gives you no clues, if your child's prospective teacher makes no comment one way or the other and if your boy or girl is fully five at the time of starting kindergarten (six for first grade), about the best you can do is to start him in school and keep a careful eye out to see how things go. Watch carefully, but not overanxiously. (Our aim is to help you see that your children are comfortable, happy and successful in school, not to make you nervous.)

But if school doesn't seem to going well, and/or if home behavior takes a marked turn for the worse, you at least have a warning. Certainly you don't have to take seriously every single "I don't want to go to school today." But if complaints and failures and trouble indicators continue, at least go down to school and talk things over. Then you and the school may, together, determine that you'd better try the whole thing a little longer. Or you may jointly determine that your child wasn't really ready and you may decide to take him out and try again next year. (Or if a junior kindergarten, four-and-a-half year-old group—or reading-readiness class, five-and-a-half-year-old group, as the case may be, is available, you may place him in that.)

The time will come, we believe, when every school system—and we hope every individual school—will have its own Developmental Examiner, as well as teachers who in addition to their natural insight about readiness will be familiar enough with the usual behavior characteristics of the age levels in question that they can easily spot overplacement or unreadiness.

Parents should always be receptive to any comment from school personnel to the effect that their child is overplaced in school, or is not ready to begin in the first place, as the case may be.

Furthermore, they should be quick to spot signs of poor school adjustment when such signs make themselves evident (as they usually will) in home behavior. They should then be quick to report such signs to the school. There should at all times be a closer relation and a better communication between home and school than is often available.

In most cases where serious immaturity or overplacement is present, both home and school will be aware of it and, working together, can usually make an adjustment which will bring about a happier and more comfortable school experience for the child in question.

But if, as is sometimes the case, a parent feels strongly that her child is not ready to begin school, or needs to be replaced in a younger grade, and the school is not cooperative, it is that parent's responsibility to stick to her guns, to be as the mother quoted earlier describes herself, "like a rock." It is your child's educational success and happiness which is in question. *You* care, even when the school may not seem to.

We have found most schools to be well informed about and strong supporters of the importance of having each child proceed only in accordance with his own growth rate. But there are unfortunate exceptions. No matter how much some parents plead and argue, some schools bring out the old cliché arguments against allowing a child to proceed at his own proper pace. Most of these arguments have been answered earlier in this book. But for your ammunition we give these arguments, and our answers to them, once again:

1. "Your child is babyish because you baby him." Very seldom is this true. Parents, and especially mothers, usually have a very good idea of what their children can and cannot do. With the exception of a few possibly over-protective mothers who do baby their children because they don't want them to grow up, most who "baby" their little boys and girls do so because these children are babyish. We consider that such parents are protecting their children from demands they are not ready to meet—not babying.

2. "He may be a little immature or unready now but give him just a little more time; he'll catch up." If the ordinary child grows in his behavior a year in a year's time he does well. Very few grow more than a year in a year, as they would need to if they were going to catch up.

3. "Repeating a child harms him emotionally and doesn't do any good anyway." No clear proof exists as to whether repeating does or does not cause emotional damage, but we have no reason to believe it does. Initial objection to repeating, when and if it is voiced by the child, should not be confused with emotional disturbance. It is not only reasonable to suppose, but it turns out to be true in actual practice, that a child who is comfortably and correctly replaced in a grade where he can do the work should (and does) forget any temporary embarrassment or disappointment at being kept back.

Repeating a grade is no panacea and it can't cure everything that may be wrong with a child. But if his problem is mainly, as so often, that he has been placed in a grade whose work is beyond him, in most cases it can do the trick.

4. "He can do the work all right if he would only try. We just have to find some way to motivate him." There are always those who believe that the secret of success, if a child is not doing well, is somehow to motivate him to try harder. The best motivation in the world for any child is not added pushing and prodding. It is being placed in a grade which fits him.

5. "But you can't put him back, he's so bright." Brightness is useful, but it is not the primary thing to be considered in grade placement. The I.Q. alone does not go to school. The brightest little boy in the world does not belong in first grade if he cannot even print his first name.

6. "We can't hold him back, he's so big." Grade placement should not be decided by the pound or the inch. Eventually, when all children are started in school, or subsequently promoted, on the basis of their behavior age, size as well as chronological age will be a secondary consideration.

7. "The children will make fun of him if he repeats." Children admittedly can be cruel. But the cruel ones will make fun of a child's size, his shape, his glasses, his race, the color of his hair, just as readily as they will comment about his grade placement. We can't guarantee that no child will ever be teased if he is required to repeat a grade. We can assure you that if his parents do a good job of convincing him that repeating (or starting later) is the thing to do, and if the teacher does a good job (if anything needs to be said) of explaining the adjustment to the class, the effect of any teasing will not be disastrous.

8. "The sooner you start teaching him, the sooner he will learn. It's all up to you." The error of this kind of thinking is becoming all too apparent as "early entrance programs" and the formal teaching of academic subjects to preschoolers fail to produce any solid educational advancement of the children so entered or so taught.

Children no matter how much they may fuss or carry on about a decision, academic or otherwise, which their parents make, for the most part do accept, usually with a certain feeling of assured security, the big decisions which are made for them.

Our sincere hope and expectation is that the day will come when developmental placement will be the custom of the country and will be taken for granted by everybody. When school personnel and parents as well recognize the importance of total readiness, when all recognize that any child no matter how bright cannot proceed in school successfully any faster than his body and his state of growth permit, at such a glorious time we will look back on our present antiquated procedure of starting children in school simply because they have reached a certain calendar age, and shake our heads in disbelief.

## PART FOUR

# Education Today

# Chapter 11

## SCHOOL CHILDREN IN TROUBLE

THERE are many boys and girls having trouble in school today whose difficulties could be largely solved by an adjustment in their grade placement. In fact, this may be true of the majority who are having school difficulty.

But no one solution, no matter how ingenious or efficient, can solve *all* academic problems. Just as with the child's physical health—the best medicine in the world isn't going to cure everybody. And also as with the child's physical health, so with children who are having trouble in school—sometimes there can be more than one thing wrong.

Those children who exhibit persistent and serious trouble with their school work and their school adjustment usually sooner or later come to the attention of the school guidance counselor, the school psychologist or a child behavior clinic. And when they do, the kind of help and advice which they and their parents receive will depend not only on the skill but also on the philosophical orientation of the psychologist or clinic. If the specialist believes as we do that since it is the child who is having trouble, an examination of the child himself (not of his family or his home environment) is in order and is the thing which will tell us most about why he is having the trouble, he will be given a careful behavior examination.

It is our recommendation, whenever a child shows difficulty in adjusting to school, that he first of all be given a simple behavior test.* If this test indicates that his school placement is wrong, as will often be the case, we would make the adjustment in grade without further ado. If this adjustment doesn't do the trick, *or* if the preliminary examination gives clues that something is amiss other than mere grade placement, we would recommend a supplemented behavior examination which will, in most instances, at least in the hands of a skilled examiner, provide a diagnosis which will tell you what to do next.

At the Gesell Institute, this supplemented behavior examination includes the following tests. First of all, the Gesell Developmental test as described in Chapter 9. We also give a children's intelligence test (Wechsler Intelligence Scale for Children).

An intelligence test, as most people know, tells the level and quality of intelligence. We also give the Rorschach and the Lowenfeld Mosaic Test and, if time permits, Thematic Apperception Test. In the Rorschach test the child describes what he sees on each of a set of ten cards which are printed with more or less shapeless "ink blot" figures. The response to this test presumably tells how the child experiences, how he perceives, what his basic individuality is like. In the Lowenfeld Mosaic test, the subject places small, colored, poker-chip-type plastic pieces on a white page to make whatever he chooses. This test presumably tells how he functions, how well he can perform in an everyday situation. Reading and arithmetic tests tell the approximate grade level of his

---

* Unfortunately at this time not every school system in the United States provides a behavior examination. All we can suggest is that if you are interested in obtaining such an evaluation for your boy or girl, you consult your school principal. If the school itself does not provide this examination, it is possible that some local psychologist, either at a clinic, or in private practice, may do so. If the school can't help you, inquire of your own physician or of any local college department of psychology. If it appears that nobody in your local community gives such an examination, here is something which parents working together, as through a local PTA, may do something about. The relationship between schools or specialists and parents is a reciprocal one. To some extent you do have to accept what services the school provides. To some extent, if the demand is great enough, the school will provide the services you demand.

performance in these two subjects. A visual test gives specialized information about eyes and the way they function.

Since some of you might be interested to learn how such a battery of tests works in actual practice, we'd like to give, in non-technical language, a description of half a dozen children typical of those who come to a child behavior clinic because of poor school work.

Some of you may have children with these same or similar problems. But even if your child's problems may be quite different from those which we present here, we assure you—most child behavior problems *do* have a clear and discernible source based in the structure of the child himself. They can be discovered, determined, described. Diagnosis is the first step toward treatment, and most school behavior problems can be diagnosed by a capable child behavior clinic, child specialist or school psychologist, using an effective battery of tests.

Some few of the details which we give here, especially in relation to some of the special tests, may seem a little technical, and we do not expect all readers to follow every detail. What we should like you to understand in each case reported is what is the difficulty, what is the special reason at the root of that difficulty and what we believe can be done about it.

*David, five years, two months, an immature boy already a behavior problem in school and clearly not ready for kindergarten.*

*Problem:* Last year David had great difficulty in adjusting to nursery school. His behavior was consistently out of bounds and he had a definitely disruptive influence on the other children. The nursery school teacher felt strongly that David was not ready to go on to kindergarten. She reported that in one fifteen-minute span he had thrown a hammer, spat at several children, dumped two buckets of water on another child's art product and urinated in a little girl's face.

His mother felt that the only reason he behaved badly in school was that he was too smart for the activities provided and was bored. Against the school's advice, and against our advice (which she had sought by phone), she did enter him in kindergarten.

In late September, David was not adjusting to kindergarten so his parents brought him in to see us.

*Test Behavior:* David's intelligence, though not remarkable, was fully normal, with an I.Q. of 103. His behavior on the Gesell tests scattered from three to five years, but centered around four-years of age. David, though normally bright, was behaving much more like a four-than a five-year-old. His Incomplete Man, for instance, included the bellybutton, which is typical of many four-year-old products but has usually disappeared by five.

His response to the Rorschach ink blot cards was like that of a four-year-old, being silly rather than accurate. In his response with the mosaic chips, instead of making something on the paper, he merely scattered pieces around, as does a two- to three-year-old. On the visual examination, too, he responded below his age— more like a four-than a five-year-old. *He* did not adapt to the test, as does many a five-year-old. Rather, the test had to be adapted to him.

*Conclusions and Advice to Parents:* David's problem is not one of intelligence. Though not specially bright, he is of good normal intelligence. His problem—as his nursery-school behavior suggested—is one of definite immaturity. He is behaving in nearly every respect like a child about a year younger than his birthday age.

His immaturity is so marked and his attention span for most things so short that should he continue kindergarten and go on into first grade the following year, serious learning and behavior problems would almost certainly develop. Here is one learning problem that can be nipped in the bud. Since David is a normally bright boy and has considerable drive and enthusiasm, at a slower pace he may do very well in school.

Actually right now he might manage in a public school four-and-a-half-year-old class on reduced attendance, but since this is not available, and he is in danger of building up a bad reputation in this present kindergarten situation which is too much for him, he will be far better off at home this year. His home situation is ideal in that he has a friend of his own age with whom he can play in the mornings, and his mother is free for afternoon excursions. However, she must have some relief from him as he is a demanding and exhausting child.

David is the kind of boy who needs time for growing. He also needs a firm hand. But most important he should not be allowed in situations that he cannot cope with. He needs to be thought of more as a four-year-old than as a five-year-old, since though he is five chronologically, he is only four in most of his behavior. He will have problems along the way but they can be greatly reduced by allowing him this slower start in the formal learning situation.

*Kelly, six years, eight months, a bright but immature boy who needs reduced attendance and a slower pace in school to relieve physical symptoms and improve academic performance.*

*Problem:* Kelly came to us in May at the end of first grade. He was on the young side, having started first grade at five years and eight months. His classroom behavior was all right, he just could not do the school work. Also, at home he had developed the symptoms of vomiting in the mornings before school and having nightmares at night.

His mother wanted him to repeat first grade next year, and the teacher admitted that he was immature and not really ready for promotion, as his attention span was short and the work too hard for him.

However, the school psychologist told the mother that she was babying Kelly, that he *must* go to school all day every day and must go on to second grade, and that he needed psychotherapy to relieve the vomiting and nightmares and to improve his school work.

*Test Behavior:* Kelly turned out to be a good bright boy with an I.Q. of 120. Though some of his behavior on the developmental examination was at his age, there were many warning four-year-old signs, as for instance his addition of a bellybutton to the Incomplete Man and his extremely poor sustaining powers. Behavior averaged at a five-and-a-half-year-old level. Reading was at a mid-first-grade level.

Response on the Rorschach was at a preschool level with correct form below three years and very restricted. Mosaic response was a rather messy four- to five-year-old performance. Visual response was below his age. In fact, to conduct the visual examination at all, procedures and demands had to be lowered to a preschool level. Visually he had great difficulty in copying from the board as he sat at his seat.

*Conclusions and Advice to Parents:* Kelly is a hard boy to plan for because his behavior scatters so widely. He is so mature in some ways and so immature in others. Also, he is very bright, even though immature. Thus intelligence is in the superior range but much of his behavior is at a preschool level.

A boy like this might do best in a tutorial setup. Since this is not available, we recommend, for the present, reduced attendance in school, and for next year, repeating first grade. (Within a few weeks after we saw him, reduced attendance and a dropping of the demand that he copy from the board had cut out *both* his vomiting and his nightmares.)

Kelly is a good example of a boy for whom a change in the learning situation, rather than psychotherapy, has already improved behavior and promises further improvement.

*Martin, seven years, five months, a boy who could not read in spite of being bright and of an apparently fully normal personality structure.*

*Problem:* Martin was a seven-and-a-half-year-old boy just starting second grade. He was an alert, engaging, handsome, masculine boy, seemingly bubbling with life, who fitted well into his family group, held his own easily with children of his own age. His teacher said of him, "We all love Martin." However, since he was unable to read, he had a great deal of trouble in school. His first-grade teacher described him as a nonreader but good in arithmetic. The school felt that if Martin could overcome his reading problem he would be a fine student, and they stated that with his good intelligence he "should" be able to read.

*Test Behavior:* Martin's I.Q. was 119. However, like many children who have trouble in school, his behavior level was considerably below his age. Most of his behavior on the Gesell tests ranged from four to six years. The Mosaic design was one of his best products, being a normal, typical six-year-old scene. But even this low general level of behavior was not enough to explain why a bright boy from a good and reasonably bookish home was so completely unable to read.

The clue to Martin's nonreading turned out to be a very poor visual performance plus a severe perceptual handicap. The visual examination showed poor acuity (not improved, as one might expect, by plus lenses). Response to specific visual tests was slow and fuzzy.

Most revealing, however, was the Rorschach ink blot test, which showed in addition to restriction and immaturity *an abnormally inaccurate way of perceiving.* Martin's accuracy of perception of the Rorschach was *below* a two-year-old level. He revealed himself as having less than a 50 percent chance of seeing things accurately. His perceptual world was clearly not a normal world, but appeared to be made up of inaccurate blobs and bits and pieces which he then combined as best he could into inaccurate wholes. Small wonder that he could not read.

*Conclusions and Advice to Parents:* Though Martin's visual performance, that is his use of his eyes, is poor, it is not in itself poor enough to account for his almost total inability to read. The root of his problem lies in the fuzziness and inaccuracy of his perception and the slowness of his response. Both of these suggest some kind of hormonal imbalance or deficiency. This probability must be checked first before visual training, which should be highly beneficial, is undertaken. (Mother admitted when questioned that there is a history of low thyroid in the family.)

Martin should at this time be put back into first grade since he is not even reading at a first-grade level. A slower course in school, shorter assignments, special individual training in the use of symbols, a check on his endocrine picture and then, probably, visual training, all should help this boy who seems to have a marked and rather specific perceptual handicap.

Discovering the extent of Martin's perceptual difficulty is not, of course, the same as curing it. However it is an important first step, since it takes his problem out of the "he could do it if only he would try" category. That is, our findings contradict the school's original comment as reported by Martin's mother that "he has such a high intelligence that he 'should' be able to read."

*Stuart, eight years, eight months, failing and behaving badly at school, being treated unsuccessfully, along with his grandmother, at a child behavior clinic.*

*Problem:* Stuart's problem was not only poor school work (failing third grade) but, primarily, uncooperative disruptive behavior in the classroom. A good boy at home and in the neighborhood, his deportment in the classroom was so rebellious and belligerent that he was on the verge of being expelled from school. For several months (prior to his coming to the Gesell Institute) he had been receiving help from a social worker at a child behavior clinic, which, since he had no parents in this part of the country, had insisted on "treating" his grandmother with whom he lived.*

Psychotherapy was not improving his behavior, and his grandmother was so upset by her visits to the clinic that her husband finally refused to let her continue. The grandmother reported that she "lost truth" at the clinic. The social worker also washed her hands of Stuart except to recommend psychiatric care for him "somewhere." The school refused to keep him unless he continued at the clinic, and since the clinic would not continue with him without the grandmother, things were at a stalemate.

*Test Behavior:* In general Stuart's record was that of a seven-year-old boy, but more than that, it was the record of an insecure child afraid to perform when not sure, and one who appeared to feel considerably threatened. However, though insecure and unhappy, he was not what we classify as "emotionally disturbed." Though there were bad episodes of behavior reported at school, he was not basically a "disturbed" child.

Intelligence was normal (I.Q. of 110). Teething, however, was only around a seven-year-level and general appearance was that of a much younger child. Behavior was uneven—he did not know such words as "palm," yet used such concepts as "disappointed." Reading was at a second-grade level. He still reversed letters and numbers in writing. The Rorschach revealed an immature boy with very strong, unmodulated emotions.

*Conclusions and Advice to Grandmother:* Since Stuart showed himself to be seriously in need of visual help (glasses), they were prescribed, and putting him back to second grade where he belonged was recommended on the basis of his poor visual behavior.

* This has been the custom in many child behavior clinics in this country. The assumption being that much of any child's difficulty is due to the way he is treated by his parents, or guardians, these adults as well as the troubled child are given help by the clinic.

Glasses and replacement back to second grade should improve school work enough, that hopefully, Stuart will not need to continue his disruptive classroom behavior. This boy needs a great deal of protection, help and encouragement. This he gets at home, and it is hoped that the second-grade teacher too will be able to provide it.

A hope that school behavior can be improved by a lightened school demand seems reasonable in view of the fact that he is reportedly an extremely "good," happy, well-adjusted boy both at home and in the neighborhood, with both family and friends. Just taking off school pressure plus visual help may do the trick. On the basis of this hope the school was persuaded to give him another try. We would delay any further therapy (since it has been so unsuccessful so far) for the time being.

However, eventually some therapy to help him get over his perfectly rational feeling that he was deserted by his parents—he was—should be given. A therapeutic situation will need to be found in which the grandmother is not required to get "help," since her husband will not permit her to continue in such an upsetting situation.

*Peter eight years, eleven months, referred as a supposed "underachiever," but actually doing well considering his modest endowment.*

*Problem:* Peter was referred because of the "mystery" of his poor school work. With a measured I.Q. of 120 and no reportedly serious emotional problems, he had already at the age of eight repeated first grade, was now repeating second and was still not doing well in school. School work was poor and, in addition, Peter constantly interrupted the class with uninteresting (to others), unimportant demands for attention. Reading "habits" were poor and he could not read or write numbers above ten. He still relied on his fingers for counting.

Many excuses had been given for Peter's poor showing at

school. Some blamed it on his enlarged tonsils and subsequent slight deafness. Others believed that he felt inferior because his older brother was smarter than he. Some felt the fact that two of his playmates had speech defects had slowed him down.

*Test Behavior:* Peter's behavior level, as measured by the Gesell Behavior Examination was mostly within the six- to seven-year-old range. He printed like a seven-year-old, copied forms like a six- to seven-year-old, read at the beginning first-grade level. He did not even know how many days there were in a week. On the Rorschach, the extreme fluidity of his concepts (a hatless, neckless man on Card II turned into a bear), and his feeling that there was a "trick" to the whole thing, gave a definitely preschool flavor. The Rorschach response also suggested a slightly abnormal personality structure.

However the real clue to Peter's poor school work lay primarily not in his immaturity but in his low intelligence. Inspection of his original intelligence test record, made available by the school, showed that the final score of the original test, which had been given correctly and scored correctly, had been added up wrong. Peter had never had an I.Q. of 120 or anything like it. His I.Q. as originally tested had been 93.

*Conclusions and Advice to Parents:* In spite of the many environmental reasons which had been given for Peter's poor showing, the true cause of his very poor school performance, as in most instances, appears to lie in Peter's own organism and Peter's own behavior.

Peter, because of his low I.Q. and his slightly deviant personality organization, does not belong in a usual school class at any grade level. He is a special educational and growth problem and needs very special handling if things are not going to get worse. He should ideally be in an ungraded class, going at his own pace and having opportunity for shop work and work along mechanical lines. He is the kind of boy who should be taught in one standard way that works with him, since he is greatly confused by alternatives. Much about him is still below six years of age.

The school has made many errors on Peter, most of which could have been prevented by a good diagnostic examination before he started first grade:

1. Considering his extreme immaturity of behavior, it was madness to start him in first grade under six years of age.

2. His I.Q. had been incorrectly measured, which confused everyone in that expectations were always much higher than anything which Peter could perform.

3. In three years of schooling it had not been appreciated that Peter's individuality was at least slightly deviant, and needed protection.

4. Three years of schooling that he wasn't ready for have been extremely confusing to this boy.

Peter is a good example of a supposed "underachiever" who is actually performing remarkably well considering his limited endowment and the too high demands which the school has been making of him for the last three years.

*Carter, nine years, three months, a fourth-grader whose outstanding problem is not poor school work but unacceptable classroom behavior.*

*Problem:* Carter's problem was not primarily academic. His school work, though not outstanding, had been adequate. His problem, or at least the school's problem with him, was his deportment. In nursery school he was considered "the biggest devil" his teacher had ever seen, and classroom behavior had not improved with the years. His constant attention-getting devices disturbed the class. At home he was overactive and demanded more than his fair share of his mother's attention.

*Test Behavior:* Carter is one of the boys whose intelligence is fully normal in spite of unsatisfactory behavior in school. I.Q. was 115, well above average. Like so many children who exhibit school problems, his behavior on the developmental examination scattered widely over a variety of ages, but much was way down at a three-and-a-half to four-year level. Growth with him appears not to have proceeded solidly and steadily but instead seems to have been made up of many little episodes, not integrated well enough that he can grow on an even front.

As with Martin, the Rorschach ink blot test turned out to give the clearest clue to Carter's problem. His response to this came as a real shock even to us, though we had realized from other tests that Carter was in rather serious trouble emotionally. His response to the Rorschach included at least seven of the eleven possible "danger signals" which we consider indicative of emotional disturbance. Even a layman, unfamiliar with the Rorschach, could have suspected from observing his response that something was seriously wrong, since it included such descriptions (of the essentially neutral blots) as "a terrible ant and blood dripping out of it, attacking something to eat."

*Conclusions and Advice to Parents:* This is a highly disturbed boy who is seriously in need of psychotherapy as soon as it can be arranged. For the rest, he would benefit by a highly structured school situation. He would do best in an ungraded private school if that can be found. His parents will need to appreciate the fact that he will not improve right away, even with the help of a good psychotherapist. If by his mid-twenties he is in adequate control of himself, they will be fortunate.

Carter is a clear example of a boy whose disturbed and disturbing behavior is based on a clear-cut emotionally disturbed personality. Thus he will need every protection that a highly structured environment can offer.

School and home have been putting up with a really disturbed boy with only minimal complaint. Important in the handling of and attitude toward a child is to know whether he has normal potentials and is just behaving badly, or is really disturbed. If the child has normal potentials, rather firm demands and rather firm discipline can be employed. If, as in the present case, the child is emotionally disturbed, handling needs to be more sympathetic and patient.

These boys—for it is more often boys than girls—are typical, in their difficulties, of the kinds of problems which children in our schools face today.

David, even in kindergarten, had he not had the good fortune to have somebody recognize his immaturity for what it was and remove him from the school situation early, might have faced a school lifetime of overplacement, and unruly behavior as his reaction to excessive pressure and too great demands.

Kelly, too, found himself in a school situation for which he was not ready, and reacted with vomiting and nightmares. The school psychologist recommended that Kelly stay in this too demanding situation and receive therapy. A developmental solution was found instead—Kelly was put on reduced attendance and he will repeat first grade.

Martin, a bright second-grade nonreader, was found to have a specific perceptual handicap. A slower course in school and specific perceptual training will, we hope, help Martin to learn to read.

Stuart, a school behavior problem, is another immature boy, struggling to do the work of a grade in which he did not belong.

Peter, a supposed "underachiever" turned out like many so-called underachievers to be functioning remarkably well considering his immaturity, his below normal intelligence and his marked overplacement in school.

Carter, of normal intelligence, had reached fourth grade without anyone having officially recognized the fact that his personality was so clearly deviant that psychotherapy was unquestionably needed—not to "cure" him but just to keep him on the track at all.

These boys illustrate most of the major reasons which we commonly find at the root of severe school behavior problems. Immaturity is, in our experience, the main cause. The majority of children doing poorly in school are overplaced. That is, they are too immature for the work of the grade in which age has placed them. Adjusted placement will help many of them.

A second serious factor at the root of many school problems is low intelligence, which surprisingly often goes unrecognized. A lower division of their grade or perhaps placement in a special class for 80 to 90 I.Q. children can help many whose intelligence is not up to the usual academic functioning.

A certain, perhaps small, number of children suffer from what appears to be a specific perceptual handicap. That is, they cannot accurately interpret what they see and thus need special individual perceptual training. Many more suffer from visual problems— problems for which, fortunately, in most instances glasses or visual training can give substantial help.

And then there is that minority who are handicapped by deviant personalities or real emotional disturbance, requiring individual psychotherapy.

For a few children the cause of unsatisfactory school work or school behavior may indeed lie in the so-often-mentioned "emotional factors in the home environment." For most, as our typical cases illustrate, the basic reason for difficulty lies in something about the child which is not functioning adequately and which needs correction or special treatment.

In nearly all, however, whatever the final solution, a careful diagnosis of difficulty needs to precede solution. We need to know what is wrong before we can put it right. An individual behavior test, given whenever there is difficulty, can in most instances provide that so necessary diagnosis.

Certainly none of you will have children who experience all the problems described in the present chapter. But some of the difficulties described may strike a familiar note.

Our main reason for describing these problem cases is to give readers a notion of the kinds of difficulties which do arise as relatively normal children have trouble in school. These brief case histories will, it is hoped, give parents an idea of things which may be giving their own children trouble.

Most of all, these histories are presented to help readers realize that no matter how complicated or mysterious a child's school problems may seem to be, in most instances a careful behavior examination given by an individual well informed about child behavior can tell you not only why your child is having difficulty but what to do about it.

And we hope this chapter has made it clear that, more often than not, the root of any child's school difficulty lies squarely in his own organism, rather than in something that you, his parents, have or have not done to him.

# Chapter 12

## PARENTS' QUESTIONS

THE questions which parents ask us about school are as multiple and as varied as the questioners themselves. We include here a selection of these questions in the hope that some of them may be the very ones which are puzzling some of you. This presentation is not highly systematic, but in general we have arranged questions in the order of the age of the child questioned about.

We do not of course guarantee that every educator of repute would answer in the same way that we have. But here, for better or worse, are some questions which have particularly interested us from all of the hundreds which parents have asked us in the recent past. A few of these border on topics already discussed; others are new to this chapter.

### TEACHING BABIES OR PRESCHOOLERS TO READ

*"I've seen a great deal lately about the advantages of teaching very young children, even babies, to read. Do you think this is possible? Do you think it desirable?"*

In some cases it is possible. In most, unnecessary and even undesirable. Of course if you have one of those "born reading" children who at some very early age shows a marked and special interest in letters and words, give him your blessing and let him go as far and as fast as his natural talent and inclination may lead him.

On the other hand, if somebody tries to sell you a book, or a typewriter, guaranteed to teach your infant or preschooler to read, our personal advice would be—save your time and your money.

It has been possible in some instances to push young children into early reading before they would have reached it on their own. Most research, such as that by Sue Moskowitz of the Bureau of Educational Research in New York City, has shown, however, that such artificial advancement is not lasting and that by seven years of age or so there is no distinguishable difference between the reading behavior of children who have been left to develop reading on their own and those who have been pushed into it early by zealous parents and teachers.

Besides not doing any special long-lasting good, even when it succeeds, early forced reading has several disadvantages. Among them, the chief one is that it definitely may not be doing any good to an immature visual equipment. And, also, children who are natural early readers are usually already spending as much time as they should at close work, by their own inclination. What they need is more gross motor and more outdoor activity. Those who don't take to early reading instruction, on the other hand, will be unnecessarily pushed and badgered by early teaching of reading, and to no advantage.

Edith Meyer Taylor of Boston, in her review of our book *School Readiness,* adds her voice to our own when she comments: "May Ilg & Ames again help to allay fears and may they succeed in adding weight to efforts of educators and mental health experts who try to delay academic learning for children not ready, and to enrich the vistas of those who can learn faster. A special prayer goes for their success in combating the forces of darkness which try to lure unsuspecting parents into teaching their two-year-olds 'to read,' instead of helping them first to see things they might later find worth reading about."

## PROGRAMS FOR EARLY ADVANCEMENT INTO KINDERGARTEN

*"What do you think about the so-called early entrance into kindergarten programs? This possibility exists in our town—that even if a child is legally too young to start school, he can take an intelligence test and if his intelligence is high enough, he can start anyway. Do you think this is a good idea?"*

Early entrance programs are exactly the opposite of what we have been recommending in this book. We think they do harm in that they arrange for the child young in years but bright in mind (what we call a superior-immature child) to be placed in a grade for which his age (and therefore in all probability his behavior level) makes him unready, even though there may be no question about his brightness.

These programs may to the uninitiated seem not too entirely different from our own. The main difference—and it turns out to be a big one—is that we rely chiefly on behavior maturity tests, while early entrance programs depend chiefly on intelligence tests. These programs are interested primarily in seeing to it that the bright young child gets an early start in school, earlier than the law allows. Our interest is rather in the other direction—seeing to it that the bright but immature young child be *prevented* from a too early start in school.

## IS KINDERGARTEN NECESSARY?

*"We are supposedly lucky to have a public kindergarten in our town—one year of school before first grade. I wonder if we would not be better off not to have it. I agree with you that children, boys especially, shouldn't start first grade until they are six. But why not just start them in first grade, when they are ready to learn, without all this time spent in school 'getting ready' to learn? How necessary is kindergarten?"*

Kindergarten is not essential, and children will live and learn without it. But we are for it, 100 percent. Here are a few of the important things which children learn in kindergarten, taken from Anne Hoppock's *What Are Kindergartens For?* published by the Association for Childhood Education International.

It is true that Nature does a big part of getting a child ready for first grade. But there is a very great deal which a good kindergarten can contribute. Some of the important things a child learns in kindergarten include:

Freeing oneself for effective work by acquiring good work habits —getting to school on time, taking care of self and belongings, using materials economically, sticking to the job, cleaning up once you're finished. All of these things, if learned in kindergarten, save valuable time in first grade.

In kindergarten a child learns to use his body more skillfully and to behave in ways which safeguard his health.

He learns, most importantly, to think of others as well as himself, to take part in group activities. Some of the rough edges of social intercourse are wearing off. He also learns to grow in independence and initiative.

Faster than he would at home, he increases his understanding of the world around him and how to live well in it. In the process he adds to his stock of information and meanings.

He learns, if lucky, that school is a pleasant place to be; that it is good to work hard; that he is the kind of person who can learn and contribute to a group. He increases his facility in communicating his ideas and feelings.

It may seem to some that the kindergarten child is just playing. But as educators often point out, play *is* the young child's work. It is his way of learning as well.

The flexible atmosphere of a kindergarten permits the child to be in school but allows him to behave at a level of maturity and cooperativeness for which he is ready. Demands can be less rigid than those of first grade, so that the child can begin school more or less in his own way, at his own pace. First-grade adjustment is immeasurably helped in most cases by the kindergarten experience.

## What Happens to Children Judged Unready for Kindergarten?

*"What if your child is presumably ready to start kindergarten but when he is examined they say he isn't ready? Does this mean that the school has nothing to offer? That you just have to keep him at home another year?"*

Not necessarily, and it should not be so. There are already some rather advanced school systems throughout the country which go so far as to provide two possible years of kindergarten. One is taught more or less along the lines of a high-powered four-year-old nursery-school group for the less mature and less ready five-year-olds; the other is a higher or more usual kindergarten situation for the more mature.

Many parents prefer to keep their children out of school entirely, or to keep them in nursery school, until they are fully ready for the regular year of kindergarten which customarily precedes first grade. But for those who prefer to start their children in kindergarten when they are still definitely on the young side in age or behavior or both, two years of kindergarten will often solve the problem very neatly.

## Is the So-Called Reading-Readiness Class a Good Idea?

*"There has been a lot of talk in our town lately to the effect that not every kindergarten child is ready at the end of the year to proceed to first grade. And so, though there has been considerable opposition, our primary school has set up what they call a reading readiness class for those children presumably unready to be promoted to first grade when they finish kindergarten. What do you think of this idea? It seems to some of us that kindergarten is quite*

*enough, without adding another extra year before the child gets to first grade."*

There are of course many mature children who after enjoying one year in kindergarten are fully ready to proceed to first grade. There are many others who need more—much more. Such children can manage kindergarten, if it is not too high powered, but they still will not be ready for first grade the following year. They need an in-between class, an extra year before they undertake the formal schooling usually offered in first grade.

*We* call this in-between class the five-and-a-half year-old class, though it has different names in different communities. Some call it a connecting class. In some communities it is called a reading readiness class. The name of course is not the main thing—the main thing is that such a class be available for those not ready to go directly from one year of kindergarten to first grade.

Having such a class available in the school setup by no means implies that everybody will need to attend kindergarten, connecting class and then first grade. In most schools only a minority of children will need the extra year. But for some, especially for those slow-maturing boys, its availability can make the difference between school success and school failure.

A Connecticut teacher, in describing such a class, has this to say:

I think people are gradually coming to realize that many normal children who have average or above average intelligence can still have a behavioral maturity below their chronological age, even though they may come from very good homes culturally speaking.

As a first-grade teacher I had watched and suffered with so many very young and unready first-graders who had difficulty in learning to read that I finally persuaded my principal to set up a transitional class between kindergarten and the real first grade.

For two years now for the less mature children in our school, kindergarten is followed by this transitional class, with only those who are fully ready going on into first grade right after kindergarten. This permits each group to move rapidly and comfortably, with no outstanding disruptive behavior problems. (So many children behave badly in school not because they are basically bad children but merely because they are lost and can't keep up.)

Within each group there is still enough spread of ability to challenge the brighter or more mature children without frustrating the less bright or less mature. The kindergarten teachers, at the end of the year, help us to determine which children should be in the transitional class and which in the regular first grade, on the basis of behavior and performance level, not merely on the basis of age or intelligence or achievement level.

We have a very informal program all year but especially so until January. The class is transitional in that I try to have an extended kindergarten program gradually working toward first-grade work. We try things together and learn.

We'd like to emphasize particularly that this in-between class definitely should not be, as it sometimes is, run as a kind of watered-down first-grade class. It's too bad for a school to spend the time and money, personnel and space, to provide this important transition year for those children who need it and then spoil the whole thing by providing more or less the very overacademic opportunity (first-grade work) which it aims to avoid. (We are also finding the need for classes between first and second grade, between second and third grade, and even between third and fourth. Six months can be a long time in the life of a child.)

## ADVANCED READING NOT NECESSARILY GROUNDS FOR DOUBLE PROMOTION

*"My daughter Carol, a first-grader, appears to be a natural-born reader. She is, right now, reading at a third-grade level or better. I think she should be at least in the second grade but the school says no, that she belongs in first grade. That's not sensible, is it?"*

It has been our finding that many children who are, as you put it, born readers are considerably farther ahead in their reading, according to the usual grade expectations, than they are in any other subject. We know of many who in reading are several grades ahead of their performance in other subjects.

But we wouldn't think of putting a six-year-old in the third or even in the second grade just because she might happen to be reading at what is considered a third-grade level. Though reading has in the past often been used as a basis for determining grade placement, it can be so far out of line with the rest of a child's academic performance, and with his general behavior maturity, that we have learned to be very wary of it as an indication of what grade a child should be in. Be glad that Carol is a good reader, see to it that she has plenty to read and let it go at that.

### DOES A PARENT HAVE THE RIGHT TO INSIST THAT HIS CHILD BE PROMOTED?

*"The teacher says my boy Joey is immature and isn't ready for first grade this fall. However, his sixth birthday is on November 5, and in our town the law is that children who are six by the fifteenth of November can enter first grade. Don't we have a right to insist that they let Joe go on into first grade?"*

If the law reads as you say, you do have a legal right to insist on Joe's being in first grade. However, if like most parents you are interested in what is best for your son, we can assure you that doing what is good for him educationally is a lot more important than insisting on his legal rights.

Any child, boy or girl, functions best and learns best in the grade he's ready for. And we can practically guarantee that if the teacher says Joe isn't ready for first grade she knows what she's talking about. Joe's November birthday would alert us at once into questioning his readiness.

The most important thing is not to get through school as quickly as possible. The important thing is to be ready for the grade you're in and able to do the work expected. Even children who say they hate school and who make a lot of trouble often become quite reconciled to school (and vice versa) if they're lucky enough to be put back into a class where they fit.

## ISOLATION OFTEN HELPS WHEN SCHOOL IS TOO MUCH FOR A CHILD

*"My six-year-old daughter Suzanne is in first grade and I don't think her teacher understands her. It is true that Suzanne is rather immature and cuts up a lot, but the teacher punishes her by isolating her from the others, and we feel that is wrong. Suzanne feels this isolation keenly, though she does admit, 'The kids don't bother me so much when I'm alone.'*

*"We have said that Suzanne should not be isolated and we have made numerous other practical suggestions for handling her in school. The teacher not only ignores these suggestions but actually seems to resent them. She says we are overconcerned."*

We can't say of course from this distance whether or not Suzanne's teacher is right or wrong in her treatment of this little girl. We CAN say from this distance that whereas most teachers are quite willing to talk things over with mothers, most of them quite understandably do not like to be told how to run their classrooms.

Isolating a child is often an extremely effective method of discipline. And many children, if things are difficult enough that they need isolation, are often more comfortable and greatly relieved by small bits of time away from the hurly-burly of regular classroom activity.

We have never favored having children sit on the floor in the hall outside the classroom door when they are bad. But if there is a reasonably comfortable place for isolation, it often really does help. We know one little boy in a small-town school who was allowed to stay in the closet when things got too much for him. (It was a big closet.)

This sounds rather odd but this boy reported to his parents, "I'm really better off in the closet. Then I don't get into so much trouble."

However, of course the real trick would be to prevent the kind of school situation in which a child needs to be isolated. Suzanne is, according to her mother, an immature six-year-old first-grader, who cannot stand the complication of the total group. It may well be that she is not really ready for first grade at this time. If she were placed where she really belongs (quite likely about half a grade behind where she actually is), isolation might not be necessary.

Let's worry more about WHY a child needs punishment and/or special handling and less about the particular method that any given teacher uses.

## TEACHER CALLS FIRST-GRADER A CLOWN

*"My daughter Chrissie is terribly unhappy in first grade for a variety of reasons. She can do the work but they say she is immature. Recently she came home all upset and didn't want to go back to school because she said the teacher called her a clown.*

*"We checked with the teacher who said she sometimes instructed the children to stop clowning around, and Chrissie took it from there. We requested the teacher to refrain from this terminology. She did not take this request kindly and felt that we overstressed the whole affair, as did the principal and the psychiatrist."*

What psychiatrist? Anyway, we don't feel that the teacher did wrong. Each teacher has her own ways of talking, and it probably comes natural to this teacher to tell the children to stop clowning around. It would likely be very hard for her to overcome her own natural way of talking.

We would recommend trying to change Chrissie rather than trying to change the teacher. Go over the whole thing carefully with Chrissie and explain that this was just the teacher's way of speaking and did not refer to her specially. (Any more than if the teacher told the children not to fool around, which teachers often do. This doesn't mean the teacher is calling them fools.)

Chrissie's distress is interesting since it illustrates the kind of trouble which first-graders, especially immature ones, often get into. Many a first-grader has refused to go to school simply because he misunderstands or misinterprets something the teacher has said. This is one reason why it's important for a parent to be in good, clear communication with her child so that she'll know something of what's going on in his mind. Often fear of school and refusal to attend is due to some tiny little mistake or misunderstanding or anxiety which could easily be dispelled.

There was the girl who was bitterly disappointed because the teacher said she wanted everybody to be present that afternoon. The girl thought the teacher was going to give everybody a present.

Or the child who had to pass the cookies in kindergarten and count them as she passed them when she wasn't sure of her number sequence. Or the child who was required to put on his rubbers and couldn't quite manage it.

Often we look deeply and give a complicated explanation to school problems when they are actually no more complicated than Chrissie thinking that the teacher called her a clown.

## HALF-DAY SESSIONS MAY BE BETTER FOR SECOND- AS WELL AS FIRST-GRADERS

*"Given the rather inflexible schedule and length of the average public school day, what is the best thing to do with a second-grader who can really adequately handle the academic side of school but who gets terribly tired in the afternoon just because of being physically immature? My seven-year-old son scores high on ability tests and really likes school work up to the point where he is exhausted and wants to be all through. Often he just puts his head down and sleeps.*

*"Do you really think that keeping him back is the answer when he is so fully up to the work intellectually? Or do you recommend letting him come home early? Or having a nap in the middle of the day? Or what? I would like to get your ideas before I get on my high horse with a lot of different ideas to present to the teacher."*

Second-graders tire, too, as well as first-graders, as you are finding out. The ideal solution might be to have only a half-day session for first-graders, and for second-graders at least through Christmas.

If and when this cannot be arranged (and often it can't be), about the best you can do is to try to get the school to agree to an occasional day off for your boy. You'd be amazed to see what a day off now and then can do for a fatigable child.

## SPECIAL CLASSES FOR THE 80-90 I.Q. CHILD

*"What is your opinion on special classes for the low I.Q. child? We do not have such classes in our school system because there is a general feeling that it would stigmatize a child to be taken out of the regular classroom and taught separately. I am not referring to children of extremely low intelligence, but just to those in the I.Q. range around 80-90, who I understand in some communities do have their own special classes."*

These are the forgotten children. Too intelligent to be in regular classes for the retarded, but not really intelligent enough to be in the regular classroom for supposedly "normal" children—all too often no real provision is made for them.

*Such children do not belong in the regular classroom.* Grouped in very special classes and taught in a different, very special way, most are able to learn many of the things which other, brighter children, learn. But they must be taught in their own way and must go at their own pace.

As one mother of such a boy explained: "Normal children can learn fast and they can learn something new every day. Boys like my son have to be taught the same thing over and over again, until they have mastered it. They could learn enough to allow them to take their own place in the adult world when the time comes, but they require very special teaching."

### HOMEWORK FOR SECOND-GRADER

*"My just eight-year-old son Timmy was such a happy boy be-*
*fore school came into his life. But no longer. Second grade has*
*been all work and no fun. He just daydreams and doesn't finish his*
*work in school. Now it's spring and the teacher wants him to*
*repeat.*

*"Homework is dreadful. He and I have the most terrible time*
*every day. He comes in from school at 3:40 and we try to do the*
*homework then. Before it is over I feel as though I had really*
*worked.*

*"He is up and down all the time, keeps changing the subject,*
*looks at the pictures in the book instead of figuring out the words.*
*If he gets anything into his hands—pencil, ruler, anything at all—*
*you might as well give up.*

*"All the time he is saying, 'You hate me, I know you hate me.'*
*The slightest criticism and he sounds like the whole world is*
*against him.*

*"But he doesn't want to repeat. It makes him feel that he has*
*worked so terribly hard for nothing."*

You say he was such a happy boy before school came into his
life. What a condemnation of school! It doesn't need to be all
that bad!

No matter how bright or slow a child may be, no matter how
mature or immature, no matter whether he's a natural learner or
not, there should be a school situation which he can fit into and
enjoy. Or at least cope with, without all this difficulty.

We can't guarantee that repeating second grade will be the total
answer for Timmy, but we'd certainly try it, since it's what the
teacher suggests. He will probably find things much easier the
second time around.

His difficulty with homework is partly his own immaturity.
Partly that many second-graders are just plain not ready for homework. No parent should be expected to suffer through homework

when her child is only in second grade. (Or in any grade, for that matter. Homework is not a parent's business.)

So many things you say about Timmy—his thinking you hate him, his blaming you because he's going to have to repeat, his acting as if the whole world is against him, make him sound to us much more like a little seven-year-old than the eight-year-old you say he is by the calendar.

As to what to tell him about repeating—try saying that you and the school made a mistake and started him too soon. And that it's going to be a lot nicer and a lot more fun when he is in the grade he really belongs in. At least try it—and good luck.

## LEFT-HANDED CHILDREN PRESENT A SPECIAL PROBLEM

*"Do you think left-handed children have more trouble in school than right-handed children?"*

It almost seems so. Theoretically a mature, well-coordinated leftie might work as effectively as a right-hander. And certainly one shouldn't borrow trouble. But if a left-handed child, especially a boy, is having great difficulty about his written work in school, a teacher should take into consideration the fact that it can be somewhat awkward to be a left-handed person in a right-handed world.

The luckiest left-handers we know are those who have left-handed teachers who can understand their particular problem and can make allowance and give the special help they often need.

## BOYS HAVE MORE TROUBLE THAN GIRLS

*"Why do you people so often say 'he' rather than 'she' when you are speaking about children in trouble? Do you mean to imply that boys have more trouble than girls?"*

It's partly just a conventional way of speaking. Since it is cumbersome always to say "he or she," many people who write about

children simply say "he" unless they are specifically talking about
a girl.

Another reason we say "he" when speaking of children in trouble is that it *is* more likely to be a boy who is in trouble. This is
true both at home and at school. Some believe that it would be a
conservative estimate to say that five times as many boys as girls
get into serious difficulty.

Nobody seems absolutely certain whether there is something in
the male organism which makes it harder for boys to grow up, or
whether it may just be that in our present culture the conventional
demands of home and school are easier for girls than for boys.

We do know that boys develop more slowly than girls do in the
early years. This, as we've pointed out throughout this book,
makes it desirable for them to be a little older than girls are when
they start in school. Since this difference in behavior level is seldom taken into account by our schools in actual practice, one
reason that boys have more trouble than girls do is that many of
them are expected to do school work they are not ready for.

At any rate, most behavior clinics, including our own, do find
that many more boys than girls are referred to them.

## ARE GIRLS SMARTER THAN BOYS?

*"Is it really true as some say that girls are smarter than boys?"*

They aren't necessarily smarter. But as we've just explained, in
the early years of life girls *on the average* do mature faster than
boys do; thus they often do better in school and give the impression of being smarter.

And while we're talking about sex differences, we'd like to say a
word about their origin. Extreme environmentalists, those who
believe that it is the culture which makes the man (instead of the
other way around) insist that boys behave differently from girls
because we *expect* them to do so. That is, that it is our expectations which make the behavior.

Certainly, expectations do influence a child's behavior to some extent. However, all of our own observations over the past fifty years or so have led to the conclusion that basic sex differences which cannot be blamed on the culture express themselves early and persistently. Space does not permit us to go into detail, but these early differences have been described at some length in *The Guidance Nursery School* by Pitcher and Ames (Harper & Row). A Brownie leader's comment may serve as a simple example to point out basic differences between girls and boys, differences which it is hard to believe could have been brought about merely by the expectations of society.

This mother, in pointing out how much easier it is to be a Brownie leader than a Den Mother for Cub Scouts, explained, "Those little boys are so dreadfully active, you have to plan for almost constant physical activity for them. With the girls, mental activity suffices and that's much easier on the leader."

Any of you who have raised both boys and girls share the common knowledge that there are many basic, inherent, differences between the sexes which it would be impossible to blame merely on what somebody expected them to do.

## SHOULD A BOY BE IN THE SAME GRADE WITH HIS SISTER?

*"Our eight-year-old David has always done badly in school. Teachers say he is very bright and could do the work if only he would try. I feel that his problem is not laziness but rather immaturity. He seems very babyish to me compared to other children of his age. He is in third grade now but he wasn't eight till December, so he is younger than most of the others.*

*"We'd like to hold him back, but that would put him in the same grade as his younger sister. How about keeping him back but transferring him to a different school? I hate to see him go on any longer in his unhappy school career."*

We always look out for trouble when a teacher tells a mother that her child "could do the work if he would only try," "is bright and could do much better than he does," "doesn't care." All of these statements are danger signals. If a child is suited to the work of the grade he is in, other things being favorable, he usually *will* try.

You ask—would it embarrass him too much to be in the same grade as his sister? We don't know for sure. But our usual advice is that each child should be placed in school where he himself belongs. He should *not* be placed in a certain grade just in order to stay ahead of a younger brother or sister.

We know that this kind of advice is sometimes easier to give than to follow, but many have tried it without any permanent disaster.

Transferring to a different school might be a good idea. Or is there any chance that they could be in the same school but in different rooms? This might be best, if possible. But even being in the same room with her would be better than continuing in a school situation which is clearly over his head.

You can go a long way with a boy by explaining that girls are often better and quicker at some things (school work) but that boys do better at many other things.

You agree with our own feelings when you realize that David would be better off in an enriched or high-powered second-grade class where he could be challenged intellectually but would still be at his behavior level. This would be loads better for him than staying on in a third grade which he is not ready for. We hope he can be in a different room from his sister but even if he can't it won't be fatal.

DOES BEING A MIDDLE CHILD PRESENT A SPECIAL HANDICAP?

*"My eight-year-old son, Dexter, a middle child, is having a dreadful time in school. He just can't seem to do the work. His behavior at home is nothing to rave about either. We can't seem to figure out the cause of his difficulty. Do you think his being a middle child could have something to do with it?"*

Almost everything about a child has "something to do with it," but we haven't observed any special set of symptoms or problems characteristic of the middle child. Many believe, and we agree, that first children, especially first boys, tend to be specially high-powered but also often are unusually complicated and do have a hard time as they grow up. We ourselves often speak of those "glorious thirds," though we don't know that others agree.

There is a general belief among parents that middle children suffer from being squeezed in between those older and those younger. It seems to us that the way a child reacts to "middleness" depends mostly on the child. There are those quiet, good-natured, somewhat retiring children who seem to enjoy their inconspicuous position. Others, more competitive, do suffer in their often unsuccessful competitive effort to do as well as their older sibling.

We personally don't feel that you should excuse school or home difficulty on the grounds of anybody being a middle child. Try instead to find out *why* this particular child is having trouble in this particular situation, and then do something about it.

### How About Summer Tutoring for the Poor Achiever?

*My boy Irving is eight years old and starting third grade. I know now that he was not ready for school when he started first grade. Near the end of the first year his teacher told me he was just not getting the work. I asked if he should be retained in first grade but she said no, just give him a little summer tutoring and he would be OK. We did.*

*"At the end of second grade I again suggested that he be retained. The teacher said she had considered it but decided against it since he was an "on the fence" case. Some days he studied well, other days not. Again summer tutoring was recommended.*

*"I have talked this over with the principal. He insists that Irving be kept with the same group in spite of poor work and inattentiveness. Says he will get better as he grows and matures more.*

*"Irving rather likes the idea of going back into second grade as some of his best friends were held back. My question is: should I*

*insist that he be put back into second grade now? Or am I a*
*foolish, frustrated mother? I have worried about this so much, as I*
*don't want another high school drop-out as his brother was. His*
*brother, too, was too immature when he started school. When are*
*the public schools going to help prevent this sort of thing?"*

As far as we know, your principal has no reason to assume that
Irving will get better and relatively more mature as he goes along.
This is, in most cases, sheer wishful thinking.

Nor do we approve of giving these nonready boys lots of summer work. We are by no means against all tutoring or remedial
help, but such help should never be used in an effort to keep a
child afloat in a grade where he does not belong.

Irving may well be one who is better at living than at learning.
However, you might be surprised at his academic success if only
he could be allowed to repeat. You have a great advantage in that
he himself likes the idea of repeating.

To answer your specific question—we do strongly advise having
him put back into second grade now. We hope the school will
agree to this. You are by no means a foolish frustrated mother.
You are one of the many who are beginning to realize that the
schools often place children poorly. And also to realize that any
child can do work within his ability better than work which is
miles above his head.

### SCHOOL WON'T ALLOW MOTHER TO HELP WITH HOMEWORK

*"My fourth-grade son, Jordan, has always done badly in school*
*right from the beginning. However, fortunately the school has al-*
*ways allowed him to bring his papers home so I could help with his*
*homework. (Actually it usually ended up with me doing most of it*
*myself, but at least it got him through school.) Now this year the*
*school has suddenly cracked down and says no more taking work*
*home. Everything has to be done in school. Of course Jordan can't*
*keep up and is failing miserably. Don't you consider this unfair?"*

No, not really. After all, it's Jordan, not you, who is trying to get through grammar school. So why should you be doing the work?

All that has been happening so far is that you've been covering up for your son. Now that he's on his own he's obviously failing. Both you and the school will have to face up to the fact that he isn't ready for the work being demanded of him. Some clear adjustment needs to be made.

## How About Social Promotion?

*"There is a good deal of discussion in our community about the matter of social promotion. Our school superintendent is all for it. In fact he prides himself that no child in his school system is ever kept back. Some of us parents are wondering about this. It doesn't seem to us that if a child is not ready for promotion, you're really doing him a kindness to promote him. Still, it seems as if our superintendent should know."*

In our opinion, social promotion is the depth of error. Of all strange notions which have prevailed in our schools in the last decade or so, this is one of the worst.

Social promotion, as most readers know, is merely the promoting of all (or nearly all) children in any grade to the next grade come June, not because they necessarily are ready for the work of that next grade, but merely so as not to hurt their feelings by keeping them back.

Nothing more ineffectual could be imagined. To put a child, or an adult for that matter, into a learning or a working situation for which he is not ready and which he cannot meet or cope with, simply so as not to hurt his feelings, is senseless.

Subterfuge and pretending and soft speaking in situations like this do not really fool anyone or protect anyone. Social promotion is like staying away from the doctor and pretending you are not ill in a case of serious illness. If seriously ill, you need medical care. If unready for promotion, a child needs to be kept back.

Social promotion is intended to keep a child happy. But no child is happy in school in a grade whose work is way beyond him. Social promotion in the long run benefits nobody. Failure admitted can be failure corrected. Honesty in school as elsewhere is unquestionably the best policy.

## NINE-YEAR-OLDS HAVE A LOT OF TROUBLE

*"A psychologist friend of mine told me recently that so far as her clinical experience would indicate, nine-year-olds seem to get into more difficulty than children of any other age. Do you believe that this is true?"*

We don't know for sure if nine-year-olds get into more trouble than do children of other ages. Some clinics do report that they have more nine-year-olds referred to them than children of any other age.

This might be due to two special causes. One, Nine is, in contrast to Eight, an age when many children are bursting out, or trying to burst out, from the confines of their families. Thus, many nine-year-olds may be trying out new behaviors which it turns out their families disapprove of.

And second, when a child is in trouble inside himself, parents often don't complain. But if his trouble consists primarily of rebelling against or trying to elude parental dominance, then parents quite naturally object, and in extreme cases seek professional help. The eight-year-old tends to be very close to his mother emotionally. Nine likes to branch out and get away and be on his own. Mothers are often made unhappy by the change. They discipline more, there is then increasing rebellion and many basically quite normal children are then taken to a clinic or child specialist.

## FATHER BLAMES SON FOR POOR SCHOOL WORK

*"Our son Kenny is failing fifth grade. He did badly in earlier grades too. But they always promoted him because they said he*

*was smart enough to do the work if he'd only try. My husband gets
very mad about the whole thing and says that Kenny inherits his
laziness from my side of the family. This makes him mad at both
Kenny and me; and makes me mad at him."*

When children fail in school, it's a natural reaction for adults
to blame somebody. Father blames mother. Mother blames the
teacher. Teacher, naturally, quite often blames the child for not
trying.

The more we understand, the less we need to blame and, fortunately, understanding of school problems and school failures is
increasing in this country. One day, we hope, nobody will have to
"blame" anybody.

### Brain-Injured Boy Does Badly in School; Mother Blames Teacher

*"My ten-year-old son, Dan, who is slightly brain injured, is now
attending a special class for such children. He is doing well academically but doesn't get on with his teacher or with the other
children.*

*"I am at a loss to understand this. He never was a behavior
problem in school before. He is very vocal and when we ask him to
explain the situation, he gives a perfectly logical explanation. He
says the other boys are fidgety and this bothers him.*

*"Also, he says if his ideas are different from the teacher's, he
should be allowed to give them, otherwise he might as well be
living in Russia. The teacher says that democracy can go only so
far in school.*

*"Doesn't it seem to you that the teacher, not Dan, is at fault?"*

Don't forget three things. First of all, when Dan was in a regular
class, the teacher and the other children were probably making
considerable allowance for the fact that he was brain injured. Most
teachers and many children are reasonably kind to children who
are different.

Therefore he may have gotten away with a lot more than he does now when all of the children in his class are brain injured and nobody makes an extra allowance for that fact. Dan says the other children are fidgety and bother him. The class may be too large. Some specialists believe that a special class for brain-injured children can't successfully take care of more than six or seven children at a time.

Second, right or not, it is the teacher who has the upper hand in this situation and if he does not want too many opinions contrary to his own expressed, he does have the privilege of saying so.

Third, don't forget that almost any bright and highly verbal child can tell his side of almost any story at home in a way that makes him seem 100 percent in the right, other people 100 percent in the wrong.

At any rate, any parent of a brain-injured child is fortunate if he can find a public school class specially suited to the problems of his special child. We hope that soon there will be many more. The special private boarding school can sometimes do wonders, but it would cost you a lot more to have Dan in such a school, and he would not be living at home. So we would advise him to try to adapt a little more at school and do his arguing and express his opinions at home.

## TEACHER COMPLAINS ABOUT BOY'S POOR HANDWRITING

*"My son Joey is ten and in the fifth grade. His teacher complains constantly about his handwriting, and most of his papers come back marked, "There is no excuse for this writing." Now Joey doesn't have very good coordination, and in my opinion (not the school's) he doesn't belong in fifth grade anyway. Also, try as hard as he may (and I think he really does try), he very seldom finishes his papers and assignments. What can I do to help him?"*

We think it very seldom that a child in school does badly *on purpose.* This is why discipline is so seldom the answer to poor school work and especially to poor handwriting. Poor school work is usually a clue that something about the school situation is wrong for the child.

A retarded reader, for example, may be incapable of successful reading achievement either due to some physiological cause, or, more likely, simply because he has been mistaught or pushed beyond his immediate capacity.

And poor handwriting is as prevalent, or more so, especially among boys, as poor reading. The reasons for this are numerous. Many boys are started on cursive writing much too early. Handwriting is not taught as forcefully as it used to be in many schools. And many boys seem to be just naturally poor writers. When handwriting is especially bad, either special help in writing should be given, requirements should be switched to a lower level or written assignments should be greatly shortened. Or, until writing can be improved, some other method of expression—such as dictating or, for the older child, typing—might be substituted.

## Is It Fair for Schools to Experiment with Children?

*"We hear a great deal nowadays about experimental schooling, from the nursery-school level right on up. Do you think it is fair for the schools to experiment with our children? Like many other parents, I have marked reservations about having my children used as guinea pigs. Also, shouldn't parents have the say as to how and when different subjects should be taught?"*

We don't know for sure what you mean by fair. Certainly it seems to us both reasonable and necessary for a certain amount of so-called educational experimentation to go on if our schools are going to improve.

Actually, most of what parents think of as experimentation is not really wildly experimental. Often it consists of no more than grouping children of some one grade into different divisions based on their response on some readiness test. Or it might consist of introducing a "connecting class" between kindergarten and first grade for those of the kindergarten class who don't actually need to repeat kindergarten but who aren't ready for first grade.

If schools are going to improve, as they're all trying to, they're going to have to be reasonably free to try out new things.

As to the second part of your question, certainly parents should feel free to check with the teacher if anything about a child's schooling bothers them, or if they don't understand what is going on.

However, teaching school is a highly specialized ability just as is practicing medicine or any other skill. Many parents are not qualified to decide just what should be taught and when it should be taught. If the parents were to decide and if, as might be the case, each parent had a different notion, pure chaos could result.

## How About Remedial Reading?

*"A remedial-reading teacher of my acquaintance told me that she was giving up her specialty and going back to classroom teaching. She said that all she was doing in her remedial-reading classes was a glorified sort of babysitting for children who were just not ready to read. And she went so far as to say that in her opinion the majority of remedial teachers were doing work which was neither useful nor necessary. Do you agree?"*

This teacher most certainly had a good point. There are a few children who because of some special personal handicap do need special, individual, remedial help with their reading.

However, our guess would be that if most children were allowed to wait till they were fully ready to start learning to read, and were allowed to go at their own pace, though many would be slow starters and would progress slowly, there would be few who would need remedial help.

Probably a large proportion of this help is currently being given to children who started too soon, became hopelessly confused and now need to be unconfused. Had they been allowed to wait till they were genuinely ready, most of them probably would not have needed the so-called "remedial" help.

Others, of course, have not even gone far enough to be confused. They are just not reading. They too need something—but it may not be a remedial-reading class.

## How to Help the Really Bright Child

*"Our daughter Priscilla is five years old. She has a Stanford-Binet I.Q. of over 190. She taught herself to read when she was four. She has been attending kindergarten in public school.*

*"We want Priscilla to have the very best education we can manage, so she may have a chance to realize her potential. We write to ask if you can help us help her. Any information, suggestions or references to relevant schools, persons, organizations, books or periodical publications will be appreciated. We are particularly interested in schools that make special provision for educating the highly gifted."*

Gifted children are without question a gift. And to quite an extent they constitute our hope for the future. However, in our personal experience with gifted children in New Haven, very seldom does one need to be treated, by us or by its parents, as a very special problem.

Most gifted children that we have known have attended good public or private schools which seem fully able to give them the enriched experience they need. Enrichment rather than pushing ahead in school is our recommendation for most highly superior children.

The danger which so many parents worry about of the bright child being "bored" if he isn't pushed ahead or double promoted is in reality very slight. The truly bright child is seldom bored in school. His busy and fertile mind seems to have little trouble in finding ways to keep him fruitfully occupied. The seemingly bored child is most often the highly verbal child with few resources of his own who needs more of the teacher's attention than can be provided. Or in other instances what parents take for boredom is all too often the response of a child who in actuality is not really up to the demands of the school situation in which he finds himself.

Thus our usual procedure is to enroll such a child in a good school, and let nature take its course. You may find that in some one field or other she will far outshine her classmates, even perhaps her teachers. A good teacher, however, should be able to take this in her stride.

If special enrichment is needed in special areas, usually a good school can either provide it or can advise you in providing it. Probably the most important thing to remember is that even a very bright little girl is still a little girl, no matter how high her I.Q. or how advanced her reading ability.

You will know a lot better just how much of a special problem (or possibility) you have when your daughter is a little older, say seven or eight. Should her I.Q. stay as high as it seems at present, you might indeed wish to make some special provision. Chances are it will level off at least to some extent.

You might like to order a book called *The Gifted: Educational Resources,* published by Porter Sargent, 11 Beacon Street, Boston. This book lists various school possibilities should you wish to send Priscilla to a special school.

However, quality education does not necessarily mean special education. Children with superior endowment should certainly be grouped with others of similar endowment in a top group. Research findings on special schools for the very superior vary somewhat, but in general show that there is no indication that the academic achievement of the academically talented students enrolled in specially enriched classes is significantly greater than that of children in regular "top" groups.

One of the most sensible comments we've heard on planning for a very highly endowed child was the comment of the mother of a highly endowed ten-year-old. She says that in answer to the oft-repeated query, "What are you going to do about him?" she replies, "Not a darn thing."

She continues, "Both my husband and I think that what our son needs is not more, but far less, academically. A child who can absorb a given topic in a fraction of the time needed by the average should then be freed, not for further academic work, but for an enrichment of his social and family life, for all-important physical development and for the exploration and development of any artistic skills he may exhibit.

"My feeling is that if my boy's formal schooling should end as of four o'clock today, he would grow up to be a sophisticated, knowledgeable, cultured adult. For he is like a desiccated seventy-two-pound sponge, absorbing and retaining anything and everything that impinges upon his awareness, whether in newspaper, magazine, TV, book or adult conversation.

". . . Failing some Utopian change in our education system, I am perfectly content for my boy to be educated along with the others in regular public school. Thus my answer for what to do with the gifted child is: *Just accept him calmly and delightedly and hope he develops into an adult who will make a good place for himself in the world.*"

We tend to agree. Certainly we would not consider it a great problem to bring up a superior child. It is not impossible, even without a large private library, to provide the books and information and stimulation which such a child needs. In fact, though we certainly don't admire mediocrity, don't think that being well-adjusted is everything, don't believe that everybody is really just as smart as everybody else given the chance, perhaps the area where the gifted child needs most help is not the intellectual (he will manage there himself) but the personal-social. The very bright child often needs help in being a more normal, well-rounded human being.

If parents could think more of a high I.Q. as a good thing to have and less as a measure of the child's total functioning, they would be less likely to fall into the trap of pushing their children ahead in school and of pushing them academically, just because they are bright.

## How About Homogeneous Grouping?

*"What do you think about this so-called homogeneous grouping, which separates the more mature, brighter or better-endowed children from those less mature or less well endowed? Don't you feel that any such grouping is undemocratic and unfair to those children who will be placed in the lower groups?"*

Some parents and some educators do consider any effort at grouping along ability lines undemocratic, unfair and apt to hurt the feelings of those children who fall into the lower group. Others, we included, favor such grouping, believing that the more similar children in any single group are as far as maturity and level of ability goes, the faster and more successful their progress in school will be.

We know of teachers in ungrouped classrooms who feel that they are teaching, in their one classroom, children who are of at least half a dozen different ability and behavior levels. Obviously such teaching is both tiring and to some extent ineffective. A whole class more or less similarly endowed, whether at a high level or a lower level, can function more effectively, more comfortably and more enjoyably.

Our own main concern is that children should be grouped according to their behavior level—that is according to the age at which they are behaving. However, we also favor for each school grade both an A and a B division, the A division for the brighter, more mature and more capable students, the B division for those who may need to go a bit more slowly or to have a somewhat less high-powered program.

Those who object to this kind of grouping often feel that it is too rigid; that a child may get in a low group in an early grade and then be stuck there for the rest of his school career. This of course should never, ideally, be the case. In any sort of grouping there should always be great flexibility. Even under very good conditions, some mistakes of grouping will be made. Or even when grouping is done with reasonable effectiveness, some children are bound to progress more rapidly, or less rapidly, than had been anticipated. There should be constant and perceptive review of any and all groupings, so that each child will not only be correctly placed at the initial moment of grouping, but will continue to be in the right kind of group as the months and the years go by. This is why we recommend yearly reappraisal.

It is very important for parents to realize that putting a child into a lower grade, or a low group, is not a matter of unfair discrimination and does not constitute an unfriendly or demeaning judgment against the child. The only fair thing for any child in school is to be grouped with others who are at the same learning level that he is. It is much, much fairer to any child to be placed in a lower grade, or a B group where he can learn and function comfortably and effectively, than to be put in a group which is above his learning level simply as a sop to his or his parent's pride.

It is as important to be in a lower group, if such is indicated, as it is to be in a top group when that is the proper placement. It is up to us—all the adults concerned—to see to it that there is no stigma attached to being in a lower division. The important thing is to allow each child to progress at his own rate.

## How About Formal Efforts to "Improve" the Child's I.Q.?

*"There are several books now on the market which advise parents as to how to improve or increase their children's I.Q. Do you believe this is something a parent should try to do? And can it really be done?"*

Such books as you refer to undoubtedly make money for the authors. We doubt that they will actually raise a child's intelligence very much. From what we know now, the Intelligence Quotient is a figure which gives a fair, though rough, estimate of a child's basic, inherited, intellectual potential. It should not be taken too literally. And if a child does a little better on a second test than on a first, it should not necessarily be concluded that he is now "smarter" than he was the first time. Rather, we assume merely that he is finding himself, for whatever reason, a little better able to express his true potential.

In general there tends to be rather marked stability in I.Q. scores from one test to another. In our experience a child's I.Q. does not actually increase (or decrease) with age in most cases. You don't by whatever effort make a child more intelligent than he was born to be. You might conceivably by various efforts help him to express himself more fully and effectively in a test situation.

Thus, in our opinion, it is incorrect for writers to lead parents to believe that they can, by reading a book and applying whatever methods it suggests, actually *increase* their child's intelligence.

### How About the Child Who Is Unusually Mature?

*"You people say a very good deal about the child who is immature. What about the opposite situation? What if a child is unusually mature for his age? In this case don't you agree that he should be pushed ahead in school, that is he should be double promoted. I feel that your emphasis tends to be rather one-sided."*

This is a fair question and one that we're glad to answer. Theoretically, since an average is only an average, there should be as many children above this position as below. And, logically, if those children who are immature should go more slowly than the average rate, those who are advanced in their maturity should go faster. That is, should be double promoted.

Here is an instance where logic and actual practice do not seem to coincide. It seems quite possible that if our school entrance requirements were more effective than they now are, and if it were admitted that, as so often seems to be the case, a child might be better off starting first grade at six-and-a-half than at six years of age, then it might turn out, indeed, that some of the more rapidly developing children might run the risk of being underplaced.

In actual practice, as we have seen it in schools all over the country in the past ten or fifteen years, with the curriculum demands of most grades somewhat *above* what the average child of the traditional age (five for kindergarten, six for first grade) is able to perform, the problem of underplacement very seldom comes up.

Though not all educators will agree with us, our experience has been that even a very bright and mature six-year-old is not too mature for the demands of the usual first-grade school experience, and so on for the grades which follow.

## WHAT IF YOU HAVE YOUR CHILD GO TOO SLOWLY?

*"What if you hold a child back and keep him out of school an extra year, or have him repeat when the decision is questionable, and then it turns out that you've made a mistake? And that really he could comfortably do the work of the grade ahead?"*

Fortunately this is not a tremendous problem. Chances are, in our experience, that if everyone concerned agrees that the slower course is indicated, this will turn out to be the correct decision.

But if it isn't, if after the decision has been made it should turn out that the child really belongs in a higher grade, happily your decision is not irreversible. If it turns out that he belongs in the higher grade, the school will almost certainly put him there.

Actually, this is one of the important tasks of the Developmental Examiner—to check on the child's actual adjustment in the grade to which his performance on the behavior examination has placed him.

In the majority of cases the placement decision is rather clear-cut and easy to make. In some, however, it isn't so easy, and only a process of trial and error will provide the final decision. But don't worry that in a reasonably flexible school system your child will get stuck in one track or another and have to stay there forever. Adjustments up or down can and should be made whenever they are needed.

How Do You Tell Your Child that He Is Not Going to Start School Along with His Friends and Neighbors?

And now a final question which deals directly with the subject matter of this book—how do you tell your child that he is not going to start school along with his friends and neighbors?

*"What do I say to my little boy when all his five-year-old friends trot off to kindergarten and he himself, at your suggestion when Dr. Ilg examined him six months ago, plus my own firm belief that he isn't ready for kindergarten, is staying in nursery school?*

*"Today was the day and though I did my best to explain, Walter cried quite a bit and just looked sort of hurt. As if he couldn't trust me. What can I tell him?"*

We'll admit that it's often easier for us to tell you what to say to your child than for you to carry out our suggestions. In this particular instance, we think we'd tell Walter that nowadays people know a great deal more about boys and girls than they used to. They know a lot more about medicine, and a lot more about school. But that not everybody knows about the new medicines, and not everybody knows the things that have been discovered about boys and girls in school.

That he is lucky that you and his father *do* know some of these new things. And that one of them is that boys like him whose birthdays don't come till November will do a lot better and will like school a lot better if they wait another year to start kindergarten.

Tell him that you and his father truly believe that school will be a lot easier and a lot more fun for him if he does things your way and waits another year. And tell him that now you'll have more time to go on excursions together. Of course to tell him all this convincingly you have to believe it yourself.

We hope that this book will help this mother and other mothers to believe as we do that each child does best in school if he is allowed to go at his own developmental pace.

# Chapter 13

## SUMMARY

EDUCATORS are now saying, "It's time that we looked at the child!" And we agree. It's high time.

In the past few decades of rapid changes in public education and rapid growth in public interest in education we have tried almost everything. Use of mechanical aids and gadgets heads the list. And then there are the various new groupings, such as team teaching, which emphasize *who* teaches the child. New arrangements of classrooms which emphasize *where* he is taught. Speed-up preschool reading programs which emphasize *when* the teaching begins. New reading and new math books abound—aimed at *what* is being taught.

But most of these programs (except ungraded primary which is a sincere though not entirely adequate effort to look at the individual child) seem to concentrate on almost everything but the child himself. To a large extent they overlook individual ability and maturity differences in the child being taught, and function as though all children were more or less the same. That is, they seem to assume that if you teach the right thing in the right way at some generalized right time, all children will or should benefit.

At any rate, the method which we recommend of determining each child's readiness for school and diagnosing readiness for any particular grade or school group by means of careful graded behavior readiness tests puts the spotlight squarely *on the individual child himself*. We need to know quite a lot about each individual child before we can know what grade or group he belongs in, what kind of teaching he needs, how fast or how slowly he will need to proceed through the primary grades.

This summary chapter, if we have written clearly and readers have read carefully, need not be long.

Our main thesis has been that behavior age, not age in years or I.Q., should be the basis for determining when children should start school, when they should be promoted and how they should be grouped. Age is important, if individual behavior examinations cannot be given, in that it tends to be the child on the older side who does best. Intelligence quotient is important in helping to decide whether a child should be in a high group or low. But ideally it is behavior age which tells us most.

We cannot expect that all readers will accept this basic thesis, but we hope that many will. There will always be those tiger mothers and fathers who will insist that their child is ready for school regardless of his behavior age and even if he misses the legal age deadline, because he is so highly intelligent. (And that he would be bored if not started right away in an advanced class.)

There will always be those others who genuinely believe that it is what you do to the child, not what he himself is, that determines how far and how fast he will progress educationally. And so they naturally will want to start their own child or children in serious academic work as early as possible—preferably in the preschool years.

Our experience has shown, however, that there is a body of informed opinion on the part of parents, teachers and administrators, all three, which increasingly respects the fact that behavior age is the most effective criterion for determining school placement, and that when this is ignored, a serious amount of overplacement does occur.

Just how much overplacement does exist in the schools today? We have hazarded the guess that from one third to one half of the children now attending primary and elementary schools (and maybe more) may be overplaced. However, the most recent guess is that of Earnest Imbach, a California educator working vigorously in a California school placement program. He finds even more overplacement than we had anticipated—from one half to two-thirds of the children entered in school on the basis of age alone appearing to be overplaced.

It is true, of course, that the curriculum of each grade, all along, *could* be reduced way down to what the children were able to perform. However, since the body of knowledge which must be covered in the schools today is greater than ever, it now seems to us more realistic and effective to work on the *other* variable—the child's ability to perform. Many curriculum changes are needed today in our primary schools, it's true. But we need *both* to improve curriculum and also to pay more attention than we now do to readiness and correct grade placement.

We can't tell you, for sure, exactly how to know if your child's behavior is immature. Some of you will have had enough experience with young children that you can easily spot immaturity when it appears in one of your own.

If you have not had such experience, check with our descriptions of behavior characteristic of the early ages which appear in Chapter 6. If your child's behavior seems more like that of a younger child than of somebody of his calendar age, you can at least suspect immaturity. Furthermore, there are certain pertinent questions, detailed in Chapter 10, which you can ask yourself about your child's behavior to give you the clues you may need as to whether or not he is ready to start school, or once started, is or is not correctly placed. If you feel that your child is immature, or is not correctly placed, discuss the problem carefully with those in authority in your school system and see if you can't arrange that a behavior examination be given.

And whatever else you do or don't do, if your child's teacher or principal or school psychologist tells you that he or she considers your boy or girl to be immature and not ready for the work of the grade in which age would place him, *pay attention to such a statement.* Try not to feel defensive. Do not interpret it that the school is saying something unfriendly or adverse about you or your child. Respect the diagnosis of immaturity as you would respect a diagnosis of physical illness.

We don't recommend that the average parent himself, or herself, attempt to give a developmental examination but we can recommend, if there is any question in your own mind as to your child's readiness for school, that you request that such an examination be given.

We can't tell you for sure how to spot immaturity, but we can give you some important warnings, many of which are implied in suggestions given earlier in this book.

## WARNINGS

1. Most important of all, from our point of view, try not to miss or ignore any signs of immaturity which you do observe in your boy or girl.

2. Don't assume that your child, if he appears to be immature as compared with others of his age, will nevertheless "catch up" with the others if given time. He probably won't.

3. Don't believe anybody who tells you that your son or daughter "could" do the work he is failing, or "could do better than he now is doing if only he would try." Our slogan is not "He could do better if he would," but rather, "He would do better if he could."

4. Don't believe anybody who tells you that it will harm your child emotionally if you keep him back. Ideally, once individual evaluation and proper grade placement programs have been instituted in all of our schools, few children will need to repeat. But in the meantime, whenever a child *does* turn out to be overplaced, he *should* be repeated. It doesn't make sense to keep a child in a grade where he cannot do the work just to avoid hurting his feelings.

5. Don't fool yourself into excusing your child's school failure or misbehavior with the alibi that he is "bored." The bright, creative child is very seldom bored in school, assuming even a moder-

ate flexibility in classroom arrangements and procedure. At least he is not bored to the extent that it seriously impedes his school performance.

6. Don't assume just because your child seems to you to be unusually bright that he necessarily requires a very special type of school or class. There is no conclusive evidence that even a highly gifted child needs to be segregated with others equally gifted, apart from other normally bright children. Certainly he should be in a top group of an appropriate grade, and should be given the intellectual stimulation he requires. But the value and need of special schools or classes for the gifted has never been conclusively proven.

7. Whenever a child is having serious trouble or difficulty in school, at least your first step toward solving the problem should be to take a good hard look at the child himself. This is not just if he is getting poor grades, but if there are other serious complaints as well. Overfatigue, not finishing papers, not paying attention, behaving "badly" in class, disliking school, not wanting to go, any of these are danger signs which should not be ignored.

Before you resort to harsh discipline, deprivation of social pleasures, or giving therapy, at least check the child himself very carefully. Is he immature? Is he substantially below average in performance? Does he need some kind of visual help? Is he perhaps suffering from some substantial perceptual handicap?

8. Don't forget that for some children it is not so much their behavior in the classroom as their behavior at home which gives the significant clue to things wrong at school. Extreme fatigue, crankiness, headaches, stomach-aches, visual complaints, expressed dislike of school or any marked, negative change from customarily happy and well-adjusted behavior can be a clue that things may be wrong at school.

9. If your child is a boy, always remember that young boys on the average develop more slowly than do young girls. Be as sure as you can be that your boy is fully ready before he starts school.

10. Keep in mind that the boy or girl who is incorrectly placed

in a grade above that in which his maturity and ability allow him to function comfortably and effectively, does not merely (as a rule) fail to do the work expected of him. More often than not we suspect that such overplacement and the resultant fruitless struggle with work which is over his head is actually emotionally harmful to the child in question. Do everything you reasonably can to be certain that your own child is not faced with such an unequal struggle.

### Things We'd Like to See in Education

1. Every child should be as correctly placed in school as possible. He should be in the grade for which his behavior, not just his age in years, makes him suitable. Thus, if he is acting like a five-year-old, he should be in kindergarten, with the other five-year-olds, even though by actual birthday age he may be six or more.

2. To make this correct placement possible, every child should ideally be given a simple behavior examination before he starts school.

3. If no such examination is available, and the child *must* be entered on the basis of age alone, be sure that your girl is fully six before she starts first grade; your boy, six-and-a-half.

4. We'd like to see our schools space grades at half-year intervals at least up to the third grade. Just that half-year would make a great deal of difference, say, for a child who is not ready for first grade but is beyond kindergarten level.

5. We favor so-called homogeneous grouping (that is, dividing the class into the more mature or readier or brighter, and the less mature or less academically able groups.) However, this should be done on the basis of total behavior ability, not just I.Q. There is many a child in a top group, placed there because of a high I.Q., who doesn't belong. Similarly, there's many a child in the bottom group of his class who actually belongs not in *any* bottom group, but in the top group of a lower grade.

6. We'd definitely like to see several different groups in any

kindergarten. Or, perhaps, a special four-and-a-half-year-old group taught more or less like a high-powered nursery-school group, for those children who would benefit from *some* school experience but who are not ready for regular, conventional kindergarten.

7. We'd like to see kindergarten run much more along nursery-school lines than it often is. And even in the connecting class which for some children comes between kindergarten and first grade, very little formal learning is in order.

8. We'd like to see half-day-*only* first grades, with afternoon time used for parent-teacher conferences and for developmental evaluation of the children when this is not otherwise provided for.

9. Special classes are very necessary for the 80-90 I.Q. child who is not adapted to the regular class instruction which fits children who are within the normal intelligence range.

10. We'd like to wait for beginning instruction in reading until the child is really ready. For some boys this age may well be eight or even nine years. Most reading failures and disabilities could be prevented if children were not started in reading till they were fully ready for such instruction.

11. A careful evaluation should be made of each child's vision before he starts school, and at reasonable intervals thereafter. Many children in our schools today are subjected to school work for which they are not visually ready. Many children who would benefit from at least temporary lens help or visual training go undiscovered.

12. We'd like to see a quicker correction of things that aren't right for the child in school. Too often a bad school situation is allowed to coast for months or even years in the hope that the child will eventually "catch up" or "straighten out." A poor school situation is as harmful as a poor health situation and should be taken as seriously.

13. And a final important thing that any of you who live in states or communities where the legal cutoff date is November, December or January (that is where children are permitted to start kinder-

garten before they are fully five, first grade before they are fully six) can do is to work on the powers that be to get this date changed at least to September first.

Birthday (or chronological) age, as we have pointed out, is not the ideal criterion for deciding the time of school entrance. But if and so long as it must be age, to have the age required on the older side is a big bonus and provides a major hope that your child will make the grade.

There could and should be a suitable learning situation for nearly every child, no matter what his abilities. Let's try to find it.

# INDEX